Collier's Guide
Night Photography
in the Great Outdoors

Text and Photography by Grant Collier

Collier Publishing

Arvada, CO

Acknowledgements

I learned most of the information in this book by experimenting with different equipment, camera settings, and shooting techniques over 12 years. However, I wanted to ensure that this book was as thorough as possible, so I scoured the web for any other tips and pointers that might be useful. I would like to thank the following photographers for the advice they have provided to ensure that capturing a good shot in the dark is more than just a shot in the dark!

David Kingham, Tony Kuyper, Floris Van Breugel, Mike Berenson, Nat Coalson, Steven Christenson, Ian Norman, Allister Benn, Royce Bair, John Mumaw, Mikko Lagerstedt, Jeffrey Sullivan, Brad Goldpaint, Thomas O'Brien, Phil Hart, Tony Prower, Marc Adamus, René Pirolt, Todd Salat, and Jason Hatfield.

©2015 Grant Collier
All photos ©2015 Grant Collier
Design by Grant Collier

ISBN # 978-1-935694-12-0
Printed in China

Published by Collier Publishing LLC
http://www.collierpublishing.com

This book may not be reproduced in full or in part by any means (with the exception of short quotes for purpose of review) without permission of the publisher.

Cover Photo: The aurora borealis lights up the night sky over Wiseman, Alaska.
Title Page: A waterfall flows beneath Kirkjufell mountain in Iceland, as the northern lights dance in the sky.
Author Page: Grant stands in the opening of Wilson Arch near Moab, Utah on an autumn night.
Back Cover: The Milky Way provides a dramatic backdrop to a ruin in Canyonlands National Park.

About the Author

Grant Collier grew up in the foothills above Denver and spent much of his childhood exploring Colorado's Rocky Mountains. Grant took up photography while attending college in Los Angeles. He found endless photographic opportunities in the Desert Southwest while driving to and from L.A.

After graduating from college in 1996, Grant began a photographic career that had him following, quite literally, in the footsteps of his great-great-grandfather, the pioneer photographer Joseph Collier. Grant traveled throughout Colorado taking photos from the exact same spots that Joseph had taken his images over one-hundred years earlier. These photographs were published in the book *Colorado: Yesterday & Today* in 2001.

In 2003, Grant began taking photos at night with his film camera. This quickly grew into an obsession, and a few years later he began shooting night photos with a digital camera. These early cameras produced large amounts of noise at night, so Grant experimented with different techniques to minimize the noise and produce high quality images. Over the years, he learned new ways of shooting and processing photos that dramatically improved his images.

Grant now produces the Starry Nights Wall Calendar, which features his night photography and includes dates of major astronomical events. He also publishes a Colorado wall calendar, featuring images from his home state.

Grant has authored numerous photography books, including *Colorado's National Parks & Monuments, Arches National Park by Day & Night,* and *Moab, Utah by Day & Night*. His images have also been featured in magazines throughout the United States and Europe.

You can see more of Grant's photos and books at GCollier.com and CollierPublishing.com. If you are interested in taking a workshop on night photography, you can join the Colorado Photography Festival, which Grant organizes each year. Find out more at ColoradoPhotographyFestival.com.

Contents

Introduction 7

I. Equipment & Supplies 11
    a) Cameras 11
    b) Lenses 12
    b) Tripods 18
    c) Accessories 19
    d) Clothing & Survival Gear 23

II. Planning Your Shots 27
    a) Software Programs 27
    b) Websites 29
    c) iTunes Apps 32
    d) Android Apps 32
    e) Moon Phases 33
    f) Months of the Year 36
    g) Twilight Stages 37
    h) Tides 39

III. Composition 41
    a) Scouting 41
    b) Foreground Subjects 42
    c) The Night Sky 43
    d) People & Man-made Objects 45
    e) Arranging the Elements 46

IV. Camera Settings 49
    a) Aperture 49
    b) Shutter Speed 49
    c) ISO 51
    d) Focusing 53
    e) White Balance 57
    f) Noise Reduction 58
    g) RAW vs. JPEG 61

V. Natural Light Sources 63
    a) The Moon 63
    b) Eclipses 64
    c) Stars 67
    d) Planets 68
    e) Meteors 68
    f) Satellites 71

g) Comets	71
h) Lightning	71
i) Northern Lights	73
j) Airglow	75
k) Zodiacal Light	75
l) Noctilucent Clouds	75
m) Lava	76
n) Forest Fires	77
o) Moonbows	78
p) Bioluminescence	79

VI. Light Painting 81
    a) Lighting Equipment 81
    b) Exposure 88
    c) Lighting Techniques 88

VII. Star Trails 93
    a) Previsualizing the Image 93
    b) Using a Film Camera 96
    c) Using a Digital Camera 100

VIII. Stitching Images 111
    a) Equipment 111
    b) Camera Settings 113
    c) Taking the Photos 113
    d) Post-Processing in Lightroom 116
    e) Stitching Software 118
    f) Post-Processing in Photoshop 121

IX. Blending Multiple Exposures 123
    a) Black Card Technique 123
    b) Multiple Shots at One Time 124
    c) Multiple Shots at Different Times 126
    d) Blending Stitched Images 127
    e) Stacking Images of the Land 129
    f) Stacking Images of the Sky 130
    h) Focus Stacking 132
    i) Enlarging Star Size 133
    j) Shooting the Moon 135

X. Post-Processing Night Photos 137
    a) Lightroom Adjustments 138
    b) Photoshop Adjustments 143

Appendix 154
    a) Resources 154
    b) Index 156
    c) References 160

Introduction

We are literally blinded by the light. The sun is so bright during the day that we can see only a blue sky above us, giving the illusion that there is little else out there. Only when the earth rotates away from this light are we able to see the dazzling display of planets, stars, and galaxies that surround our tiny planet.

For a long time, it was very difficult for the average photographer to capture good images of this celestial display. Film simply wasn't light sensitive enough to capture high quality images with short exposures. The digital revolution has changed all of this. With a little practice, anyone can now capture stunning images of the night sky with relatively inexpensive equipment.

Astronomers with massive telescopes can still capture far more distant objects than we are able to with standard lenses on a DSLR. However, these lenses can do something that powerful telescopes cannot. They can capture terrestrial objects in the foreground, giving context to the scene and tying everything back to our home planet.

When we capture images of the night sky, we are able to capture objects spread out over immense distances. When shooting such distant objects, we are not just photographing different points in space; we are also capturing different points in time. The universe is so vast that some of the photons of light that reach the camera sensor have been traveling through the vacuum of space for hundreds, thousands, or even millions of years.

Our nearest celestial neighbor is the moon, which is a mere 240,000 miles away. Light from the moon takes a little over a second to reach us. So when you photograph the moon, you are peering back one second into the past. Light from Venus, which is the brightest planet in the sky and the closest one to us, takes between 3-13 minutes to reach us, depending on where it is in its orbit relative to Earth. The second brightest planet in the night sky is Jupiter, the largest of all the planets. Light from this gas giant takes 35-52 minutes to reach us. The most distant planet in our solar system is Neptune. It appears as a tiny speck of light in the sky, indistinguishable from the stars around it. Light from this planet takes four hours to reach Earth.

While these distances are immense, they are nothing compared to the stars. Light from the nearest star, Proxima Centauri, takes a little over four years to reach Earth. Light from the most distant star we can capture using a wide angle lens under relatively dark skies departed over 16,000 years ago. At this time in Earth's history, the great Egyptian pyramids had not yet been built. Earth was still gripped in the last ice age, and humans lived as primitive hunters and gatherers.

Since it takes so long for the light to reach us, there's a chance that one of the stars you capture in a photograph no longer exists. If it was large enough, it might have exploded in a massive supernova. The dazzlingly bright light from that supernova, however, may not reach Earth for many more centuries or millennia.

The stars that we can capture in a photograph make up only a small portion of the Milky Way Galaxy, which is 100,000 light years across. We can, however, still peer much farther back in time. A standard digital SLR can easily record light from the Andromeda Galaxy. This galaxy is an unfathomable 15,000,000,000,000,000,000 (15 quintillion) miles away.

When light left this galaxy 2.5 million years

Left: The Milky Way rises above bizarre rock formations in Utah's San Rafael Swell. The Andromeda Galaxy is visible near the upper right. Canon 5D II, 24mm, f2.0, 30 seconds, ISO 6400.

ago, Homo sapiens had not yet evolved. In fact, our most distant ancestors in the Homo lineage, known as Homo habilis, would not evolve for at least 100,000 more years.

The nearest galaxies are the most distant objects we can capture with standard camera gear. However, even this represents only a tiny fraction of the size of the universe. There are approximately 200 billion galaxies stretched over unimaginably vast spaces. Light from the most distant galaxy ever observed with the Hubble Space Telescope departed over 13 billion years ago. At this time, the universe was a mere 800,000 years old, and it would be billions of years before the sun and Earth formed.

Digital cameras allow photographers to capture detailed photographs of some of these unfathomably distant objects. However, it requires a lot of expertise to capture these images, as the rules of photography are oftentimes turned on their head.

When I first started taking photos at night in 2003, I was faced with the challenge of learning these rules with equipment that was fairly primitive compared to what we have today. I used a film camera with superfine grain ISO 100 film to capture very long exposures that resulted in star trails. If I had attempted shorter exposures to render the stars as points of light, the images would have been vastly underexposed and almost unusable. Film with an ISO of 800 or 1600 would have worked better for short exposures, as it is more light sensitive. However, this film is very grainy and doesn't result in very good quality images.

In 2006, I started shooting night photos with my new Canon 5D digital camera. I was able to capture short exposures at night that were superior to what I could obtain with a film camera. However, these early digital cameras produced large amounts of noise at night, and it was still difficult to capture photos with a lot of detail. I had to experiment with many different camera settings and lenses to discover what worked best. Eventually, I began creating huge stitched images to minimize the noise that was so problematic with early digital cameras. I also experimented with equatorial mounts, which allowed me to take much longer exposures while still rendering the stars as round points of light. Any foreground in these images was blurred by the movement of the mount. However, digital imaging software had also improved to the point where I could combine a separate image of the foreground with an image of the night sky.

Once I captured the images on camera, I was faced with the challenge of optimizing them on the computer using Adobe Photoshop or Lightroom. Night photos can be more difficult to process than daytime photos, as they often look very flat and have a lot of noise. Over time, I developed a workflow that helped me minimize noise and bring out the colors and details in the night sky.

With the improvement of digital cameras, night photography has become increasingly popular. Places that I once had to himself at night, like Arches National Park, are often filled with photographers trying to capture dramatic images of the night sky. However, there is still limited information on how to capture these nightscapes. Much of this information is scattered throughout the web. It's difficult to know what information you should rely on, as some of it is accurate and some is not. So I decided to share just about everything I have learned over the past 12 years in this book.

This book is intended for those who already have a good understanding of how to use a digital SLR camera. You should know how focus manually, how to get a proper exposure when shooting in manual mode, and how to view and interpret the histogram. I won't spend a lot of time going over the basics, as there are a lot of books that cover this. I want to focus on the things that are unique to shooting at night and that are not easy to learn elsewhere. A good resource for learning the basics is Nat Coalson's book *Nature Photography Photo Workshop*.

My book is also intended for those with a fundamental understanding of how to process images in Photoshop and/or Lightroom. You should know how to import photos into Lightroom and adjust them in the Develop module (alternatively, you can make the same adjustments in Adobe Camera Raw). You should also know how to use layers in Photoshop and make selections and masks. Again, I will focus on specialized post-processing techniques that are geared towards night photography. Nat Coalson has co-authored a great book with Rob Sylvan called *Lightroom 5: Streamlining Your Digital Photography Process*. Also, Jan Kabili produces a lot of excellent videos and books on how to process images. I particularly recommend her new book *Adobe Lightroom and Photoshop for Photographers Classroom in a Book*.

Although these resources are helpful, the best way to learn is through practice. It's easier to learn when shooting during the day, as getting good quality shots at night can be much more difficult. However, if you are fairly new to photography and still want to jump right into night photography, I recommend starting with Chapters I-VI. These chapters mostly go over the basics of night photography. You can then skip to Chapter X on post-processing images at night. The section on Lightroom Adjustments in this chapter is fairly basic, but the section on Photoshop Adjustments is more advanced. Once you're comfortable with this material, you can tackle Chapters VII, VIII, and IX. These chapters cover more and more advanced topics, with Chapter IX being suitable for the most experienced photographers.

The last few chapters discuss some advanced post-processing techniques. For those who want an in-depth demonstration of all of these techniques and a few new ones, I've created a video on post-processing night photos. It is available for purchase at http://www.collierpublishing.com.

In both this book and the video, I discuss many different ways of capturing and processing photos, from taking single exposures to combining multiple exposures. Some people may object to combining multiple exposures, as they believe it makes the images "less real." However, you will oftentimes need to combine multiple exposures to reduce noise and increase the quality of the images. Since noise is an unnatural artifact in images, it is not "real." So it could be argued that some images from multiple exposures are more "real." Ultimately, it comes down to your definition of reality and how close you want to keep your images to that reality.

Some people may define reality as that which we can see with our own eyes. If a photograph doesn't closely match that, it is not "real." This is, however, nearly impossible to accomplish with night photos. The camera can capture far more stars than the eye can see. Just because the stars are not visible to the naked eye does not make them any less real.

Also, cameras are designed to create images that mimic how we see during the day. We see much differently at night. This is because we see mainly with rods in our eyes at night vs. cones during the day. Rods are far more light sensitive, but you can't see nearly as much detail with them. Rods are more sensitive to blue and green wavelengths of light than to reds. However, you cannot see color with rods, and unless you have a bright light source that can be seen with cones, the world at night appears black and white.

Cameras, on the other hand, still capture things at night the way we would see them with cones, since that's how they were designed. No DSLR camera is able to capture things as we see them with rods. In post-processing, we could try to dramatically subdue the colors and details in an attempt to mimic what we see with rods. This would produce rather dull, monochromatic images. Alternatively, we can bring out the colors and try to mimic how we would see if our cones were incredibly light sensitive. I choose the latter, as I think it's fascinating to know all the colors and details the camera can "see" at night that we can't.

Ultimately, there really is no fixed reality. We all have different ways of interpreting what exists at night. To some extent, we can only imagine what the night sky looks like, as we are half-blind to it. The camera can help bring our imagination to life.

I. Equipment & Supplies

Today, photography equipment is so advanced that about any modern digital camera can produce great images when shooting photos during the day. Owning the right equipment is still of some importance and can increase the options available to a photographer. However, the quality of the images depends mostly on the talent of the photographer, not on the equipment they are using.

While the talent and knowledge of the photographer is still of great importance when taking photos at night, owning the right equipment becomes much more valuable. The proper equipment can help minimize noise that is inherent in low-light images and make it possible to print these images at large sizes.

Image noise is an unnatural variation in color or brightness of an image. It can be produced by the circuitry in a digital camera or by the random nature in which photons hit the camera sensor. It exists in all images but is essentially drowned out during the day because of the large number of photons hitting the sensor. At night, so few photons hit the sensor that the noise competes strongly with the signal and can greatly reduce the quality of the images. Minimizing this noise is one of the biggest challenges of night photography and is something that will be discussed extensively throughout this book.

The first step in the battle against noise is using the right equipment. You don't necessarily need to spend a fortune on this equipment. A newer digital SLR camera and one or two fairly inexpensive lenses can be all you need to capture stunning images at night.

In this chapter, I'll provide a summary of the equipment that I find most useful for shooting at night. Since equipment is constantly changing, I recommend that you do some research online before purchasing anything. DxOMark.com is one of the best sites for evaluating equipment, as it extensively tests and rates many different cameras and lenses. You can find reviews of equipment on many other websites, and a lot of these will have opposing viewpoints. However, I tend to trust DxOMark more than most sites, as they attempt to do rigorous, unbiased testing of the equipment. The tests, however, aren't designed specifically for night photography, so the ratings aren't perfect.

In order to keep the information I provide current, I'll keep an updated list of equipment that I recommend for use in night photography at http://www.gcollier.com/gear/. Since digital cameras become outdated faster than anything else, I'll only discuss them briefly in this book. I recommend checking this website before purchasing a new camera.

CAMERAS

Digital cameras have improved dramatically in the past decade, allowing you to capture high quality images with short exposures at night. However, film cameras can sometimes still be preferable for taking long exposures, which result in star trails. I will therefore discuss both types of cameras.

Digital Cameras

DxOMark.com rates cameras based on their color depth, dynamic range, and low-light ISO. The most important rating for night photography is low-light ISO performance. This is called Sports (Low-Light ISO) on DxOMark. However, you can ignore the Sports designation, as low-light ISO is at least as important for night photography as it is for sports.

Currently, Nikon cameras that are rated best for low-light ISO performance include the Df, D3s, D4s, D610, D750, D800, D800e, and D810. The Canon EOS cameras rated best for low-light ISO performance are the 1Dx, 6D, and 5D Mark III. For those

---

Left: A dramatic display of the northern lights is reflected in a lake near Yellowknife, Canada. By using one of the top-rated cameras for low-light ISO performance and a Nikkor 14-24mm lens, I was able to capture a high-quality image with a single exposure. Nikon D800e, 14mm, f2.8, 15 seconds, ISO 2500.

wanting a lighter camera, the Sony A7R and A7S are compact, mirrorless cameras that are rated very well in low light. Although each of these cameras performs a little differently at night, you really can't go wrong with any of them. If you're on a tight budget, I recommend the Canon 6D or Nikon D610, both of which can be purchased for well under $2,000.

If you already own a digital SLR that is not rated as high for low-light ISO performance, I don't necessarily recommend going out and buying a new camera. Most modern digital SLRs can produce good results at night. If you use a fast lens and the techniques outlined in this book, you can still achieve excellent results. Most of the photos in this book were taken with the Canon 5D Mark II, which is no longer considered top-of-the-line for night photography. However, by stitching together multiple images, as described in Chapter VIII, I have made huge, high-quality prints of night photos taken with this camera. So it may be better to use the camera you currently own as you become proficient in night photography. If you decide your camera is not producing the quality of images you want, you can consider an upgrade.

Film Cameras

Although few photographers still shoot with film cameras, I've found them to be useful when shooting star trails at night. I'll discuss this in detail in Chapter VII. I recommend reading this chapter before purchasing a film camera. I'll review different film cameras and go over the advantages and disadvantages of shooting film vs. digital for star trails.

Film cameras aren't very useful for shorter exposures at night, as you would have to use film with a very high ISO. High ISO film is very grainy and can produce results that are inferior to a digital camera.

When shooting with film, you will get the best results with a camera that uses larger film, such as a medium format, 4x5, or even 8x10 camera. However, this can be quite expensive and may not be worthwhile just for shooting star trails. For most photographers, it is probably more practical to buy a 35mm SLR film camera that is compatible with the lenses that you use with your digital camera. These cameras can often be found on eBay for around $50.

35mm cameras will produce images with more grain, but I've found that the noise reduction software I discuss in Chapter X (Topaz DeNoise) also does a good job with reducing grain.

I captured this image of star trails over Balanced Rock in Arches National Park with an inexpensive film camera I purchased on eBay. Canon EOS 650, 24mm, f2.8, 4 hours, ISO 100.

LENSES

Owning the right combination of lenses is perhaps even more important for night photography than owning the right camera. You need lenses with wide apertures that can let in a lot of light. I recommend lenses that have apertures at least as wide as f2.8. These lenses will help minimize noise, but there are also pitfalls you should be aware of when shooting with such fast lenses.

One problem with lenses with wider apertures is that they will often produce coma in the corners of the images. In night photos, coma will make stars look like birds with wings rather than points of light. Lenses with aspherical elements are generally better at reducing coma. However, depending on how they are built, even these lenses can produce a lot of coma. Also, the price of the lens is rarely indicative of how well it will perform in low light with wide apertures. Many of the most expensive lenses will show a lot of coma, while some of the less expensive options can produce superior results.

A couple other problems you may have with lenses when shooting at night are chromatic aberration and vignetting. In night photos, chromatic aberration will generally appear as an unnatural color fringe around the edge of stars. Vignetting will cause the corners of the image to appear darker than the rest of the image. These issues can be more easily corrected in post-processing than coma, but it is still best to find lenses that keep these problems to a minimum.

I've listed some lenses that work well for night photography and can help minimize coma, chromatic aberration, and vignetting. I've included a large number of lenses for those wanting as much versatility as possible. However, you don't need all of these lenses. If you're new to night photography and are looking to buy just one lens, I'd recommend starting with the Rokinon 14mm. If you want to try stitched images, I recommend one of the 35mm or 50mm lenses that I've listed. These are really the only lenses you need to capture a wide variety of stunning night photos.

14mm Lenses

When I am not stitching together multiple images, I usually use an ultra-wide 14mm f2.8 lens. This lens captures a very wide field of view, which is important when photographing something as vast as the night sky. It also gives you a lot of depth of field, even at the widest apertures. At f2.8, you can render objects in focus from about four feet to infinity (more info will be provided on focusing and depth of field in Chapter IV). Two 14mm lenses I recommend are:

Rokinon/Samyang/Bower 14mm f/2.8

This lens can be used with virtually any digital SLR, as there are versions of it for many different camera models, including Canon, Nikon, and Sony. The lenses made by this company are marketed under many different names, including Rokinon, Samyang, Bower, Pro Optic, and Vivitar. Regardless of the name used, all of the lenses are identical. Sometimes one brand name will be priced lower than another, so I recommend purchasing the lowest cost version.

The Rokinon 14mm is a very good lens that renders sharp detail throughout the image and minimal coma at wide apertures. It can be purchased for around $300. It doesn't have the versatility of the Nikkor 14-24 that I'll describe next, but it is a much more affordable option that can produce great images at night. Rokinon lenses do not support autofocus, and you have to manually set the aperture. However, this is not very important for night photography. You'll need to know how to manually focus your lens when shooting at night anyway, and you'll usually just leave the aperture set at f2.8.

Nikon Nikkor 14-24mm f/2.8

This is probably the best ultra-wide zoom lens that has ever been made. It outperforms virtually all of the fixed focal-length wide angle lenses. You can purchase the Novoflex EOS/NIK-NT Lens Adapter to use it on a Canon. This lens retails for around $2,000, making it less suitable for those on a budget. However, if you want the versatility of a zoom lens and the best quality, you can't go wrong with the Nikkor. I find it useful not just for night photography but for many photos I take during the day.

20mm Lenses

I have personally found that a 20mm lens often won't be wide enough for single exposures and will be too wide to create very large stitched images. I therefore don't recommend buying this lens if you are new to night photography. However, if you discover that it fits your style of shooting, there are a couple options available.

Sigma 20mm f/1.8

As with many of the Sigmas, this is a high quality lens that can produce good results at night. It can be purchased for around $550.

Nikon Nikkor 20mm f/1.8G

This is a new lens that came out right before this book went to print. Initial reviews are positive. It does, however, cost $250 more than the Sigma. I'll provide more info on this lens as it becomes available at: http://www.gcollier.com/gear/.

The northern lights dance above Wiseman, Alaska. My Nikkor 14-24mm lens was invaluable for capturing a large portion of the sky. Canon 5D II, 14mm, f2.8, 15 seconds, ISO 6400.

24mm Lenses

The first lens I purchased for my night photography was a 24mm lens with a very wide aperture. However, I didn't use it as much as I expected. I found that it often wasn't wide enough for single exposures, and my 50mm lens created larger, higher quality stitched images. However, with the 50mm lens, you will have to stitch together as many as 100 images to get the full band of the Milky Way in the image. If you don't have the patience for this or if your computer doesn't have the processing power, a 24mm lens can be good for making smaller stitched images. A 24mm lens can also be useful for single exposures, as you won't always want to go as wide as 14mm.

A 24mm lens also provides more depth of field than a 35mm or 50mm lens. With a 24mm lens at f1.8, you can get objects in focus from 18 feet to infinity. If you stop down to f2.8, you can get objects as close as 11 feet away in focus.

If you choose to buy the Nikkor 14-24 mentioned in the previous section, you likely won't need a fixed 24mm lens. The Nikkor 14-24 doesn't have as wide of an aperture as some of the fixed lenses, but you can still get very good images at night with it at 24mm.

A fixed 24mm lens I recommend is:

Rokinon/Samyang/Bower 24mm f/1.4

As with the 14mm lens, the Rokinon 24mm manual-focus lens is a great lens for night photography. It has aspherical elements that minimize coma, and it can be purchased for around $550.

35mm Lenses

You may occasionally use a 35mm lens to take a single, short exposure at night. However, you'll likely find that the night sky and the Milky Way are so vast that 35mm isn't wide enough to capture as much of the night sky as you would like with one exposure. Also, as I will discuss in Chapter IV, you need to take shorter exposures with longer lenses in order to capture the stars as round points of light. Shorter exposures will result in images with more noise.

You will likely find a 35mm lens much more useful for creating stitched images. I used to prefer a 50mm lens for stitching, as it allowed me to create images that were twice as large as ones taken with a 35mm lens. However, you also have to take twice as many images with a 50mm lens, which can be a tedious and time-consuming task. As cameras have improved, I've found that I don't need quite as large stitched images to get really good quality images at night. So a 35mm lens is well suited for stitched images, and it also provides more depth of field than a 50mm lens. With a 35mm lens at f1.8, you can get objects in focus from about 40 feet to infinity.

35mm and 50mm lenses can also be used to capture star trails. You won't always need an ultra-wide lens for this, as the lines streaking across the image will look similar regardless of the focal length you use.

The 35mm lenses I recommend are:

Rokinon/Samyang/Bower 35mm f/1.4

As with most Rokinon lenses, the 35mm manual-focus lens is a great product in terms of price and quality. It can be purchased for around $400.

Sigma 35mm f/1.4

This lens has a higher DxOMark score than the Rokinon, but it does cost about twice as much. It also has autofocus. Although autofocus is not necessary when shooting at night, it can be used to focus on the moon or on a flashlight placed at a set distance. I will discuss this in more detail in Chapter IV.

50mm Lenses

I recommend a 50mm lens with a maximum aperture of at least f1.8. As mentioned before, this lens is useful for taking very large stitched images, which will allow you to overcome many of the problems with noise. One disadvantage of a 50mm lens is that you get little depth of field at wide apertures. With the lens set at f1.8, you can only get objects in focus from about 80 feet to infinity. You are therefore not able to include close foreground objects in the scene as they will be rendered out of focus.

You can get around this problem if you shoot multiple frames with different focus points for each shot in the stitched image. You can later blend all of the images with different focus points using stacking techniques described in Chapter IX. Then, after you've focus stacked all of these images, you can stitch them together. This is, however, a difficult and tedious task, and I recommend avoiding it if possible. It is much easier to do a smaller stitched image with a wider lens that provides more depth of field.

For those on a budget, there are some inexpensive 50mm lenses with wide apertures that can work well for stitching images. These lenses can produce a lot of coma in the corners. However, since I generally only use a 50mm lens for stitched images, I've found a simple way around this. I simply crop off the corners before stitching the images. This will also minimize any vignetting in the image. This process will be explained in more detail in Chapter VIII.

For those willing to pay a little more, I recommend:

Rokinon/Samyang/Bower 50mm f/1.4

This lens was introduced late in 2014, and it should be available for purchase by the time this book is in print. Given the quality of other Rokinon lenses, I'm confident that this will be a very good lens for night photography. It will retail for around $550.

For Canon shooters on a budget, I recommend:

Canon EF 50mm f/1.8 II:

This is a remarkably good lens that is available for just $125. According to DxOMark.com, it outperforms the $400 Canon 50mm f1.4 and the $1500 Canon 50mm f1.2L. The latter two lenses have a wider maximum aperture. However, you will also get more coma when shooting at such wide apertures. While the coma can be minimized by cropping out the corners, you may not get rid of it entirely. So this less expensive option is truly a great value.

For Nikon owners, there are a couple more options:

Nikkor 50mm f/1.8D

Like the Canon 50mm f1.8, this is a very high quality, low cost lens that retails for around $100. You do have to manually set the aperture on this lens.

Nikkor 58mm f/1.4G

This lens was built by Nikon with night photography in mind. It was specifically designed to minimize coma and vignetting in the images, even at f1.4. It does come with a hefty price tag of around $1,700, but it might be worth the cost if you want to capture very large stitched images with superior quality.

85mm Lenses

An 85mm lens can be used to create huge stitched images at night. It is probably the longest lens I would recommend for stitched images. With longer lenses, the stars may move too much relative to the foreground during the time it takes to capture all of the exposures. Even with this lens, you would need to take all of the images as quickly as possible to avoid too much star movement. It will also provide little depth of field. At f1.8, you can get objects from 225 feet to infinity in focus.

I only recommend this lens for creating stitched images if you are an experienced photographer who wants to make very large prints of the highest quality. A 35mm or 50mm lens will be more than adequate for most stitched images.

An 85mm lens I recommend is:

Rokinon/Samyang/Bower 85mm f/1.4

This is another very high quality, manual-focus lens made by Rokinon that is available for just $300.

Fisheye Lenses

Fisheye lenses can capture an even wider view of the sky than a standard 14mm lens. However, they significantly distort the image and can turn a flat hori-

The Milky Way rises above Fisher Towers near Moab, Utah. I used a 50mm lens to take 28 shots of portions of this scene. I later stitched all of the images together. Canon 5D II, 50mm, f1.6, 10 seconds, ISO 6400.

zon into a curved horizon. I usually prefer a standard 14mm lenses to capture wide swaths of sky. These lenses can still distort an image but not nearly as much as a fisheye. If I want a wider field of view, I generally prefer to create a stitched image rather than use a fisheye.

There are two types of fisheye lenses - a circular fisheye and a diagonal fisheye. A circular fisheye usually captures a full 180-degree field of view, though some can capture an even wider field of view. This lens is called a circular fisheye because it renders the image as a circle with a black border around it.

A diagonal fisheye produces standard, full-frame rectangular images. It usually captures a 180-degree field of view diagonally from corner to corner but not across the entire image.

One interesting use of a circular fisheye is that if you point the camera straight up, you can capture the entire night sky, and the horizon will be rendered as a circle around the edge of the image. This can produce some unique and interesting images. Whether this makes it worth the cost of a fisheye is up to each photographer. If you're unsure, I'd recommend renting one and trying it out first.

Two fisheye lenses I recommend are:

Sigma 8mm f/3.5 Circular Fisheye

If you're looking for a circular fisheye, the Sigma, which costs around $900, can produce excellent images at night.

Rokinon/Samyang/Bower 12mm f/2.8 Fisheye

This diagonal fisheye is another new lens announced by Rokinon that should be of high quality. The price and release date hadn't been announced when this book went to print.

Telephoto Lenses

If you're looking to capture dramatic shots of the night sky that include foreground objects here on Earth, you likely won't have much use for a telephoto lens. However, telephoto lenses can be useful for capturing things like lava or forest fires, which you often can't get close to at night.

You can also use a telephoto lens with an equatorial mount to capture detailed images of a small part of the night sky. This can be especially useful when photographing lunar eclipses. I'll discuss this in more detail in Chapter IX. You can capture even more distant objects by mounting a camera onto a telescope. This can allow you to capture some truly stunning images, but it takes a lot of technical expertise and is outside the scope of this book.

Telephoto lenses with wide apertures can be very expensive and probably aren't worth the cost to be used solely for night photography. If you already own one for wildlife photography, it can be fun to occasionally use at night. Otherwise, there are less expensive options with smaller apertures that can still produce good quality images.

A telephoto lens I recommend is:

Tamron 150-600mm f/5.0-6.3

This lens can be purchased for around $1,000, making it a great value for a telephoto lens. The quality isn't as good as some of the high-end prime lenses. However, if you want a 500mm f4.0 lens made from Nikon or Canon, you'll be paying around $10,000.

Lenses for Cropped Sensors

If you are using a camera with a cropped sensor and want to purchase lenses for night photography, I recommend the lenses discussed previously in this chapter. These can be used on cameras with cropped sensors but will also be useful if you decide to upgrade to a camera with a full-frame sensor. Cameras with full-frame sensors are quite a bit better for night photography, as the larger surface area of the sensor allows you to capture images with less noise.

If you use a standard lens on a camera with a cropped sensor, you won't get as wide a field of view as you would with a full-frame camera. If you prefer an ultra-wide angle lens made for a cropped sensor, I recommend:

Tokina 11-20mm f/2.8 DX

Shortly before this book went to print, it was announced that this lens will be replacing the Tokina 11-16mm f2.8 II, which is a great lens for night pho-

Since it was too dangerous to get close to the lava flowing into the Pacific Ocean from Hawaii's Big Island, I used a telephoto lens to capture this shot. Canon 5D, 300mm, f5.6, 30 seconds, ISO 400.

tography. I expect the new lens to improve on that one. There are versions of these lenses for Canon, Nikon, and Sony cameras.

TRIPODS

While you can sometimes get away with not using a tripod during the day, you have to use a tripod at night. You'll be shooting long exposures that cannot be handheld without blurring the image.

Tripod Legs

Carbon fiber tripod legs have become standard for most professional photographers, since they are very strong and lightweight. While they can be expensive, they are well worth the cost. Gitzo produces some of the most durable tripod legs, and I use one as my primary tripod. For a less expensive option, I also recommend the Feisol carbon fiber tripods.

If you are tall, make sure and get a tripod that is high enough to use without stooping over. Never rely on the center bar on the tripod to raise it higher, as this will make the camera much less stable. If possible, I recommend purchasing a tripod that doesn't have a center bar, as all it really does is add extra weight.

If you choose to shoot with a film camera as well as a digital camera, you might consider a light second tripod to use with your film camera. Since 35mm film cameras tend to be lighter than digital SLRs, the smaller tripods and ball heads can support them if used with a lighter lens.

Ball Heads

I recommend getting a ball head that has a rotating base with degree markings on it. This will make it much easier to create stitched images at night. I use the Acratech Ultimate Ballhead, as it is a top-of-the-line ball head and is very durable and lightweight. This ball head costs around $300, but I've found that less expensive ball heads don't last very long if you put them to heavy use. If this ball head is out of your price range, a less expensive option is the Manfrotto 498RC2, which costs about $100. I use this ball head on my second tripod, which doesn't get nearly as much use, and it has worked well so far.

ACCESSORIES

In addition to the camera, lens, and tripod that you use, there are many accessories that are important for night photography.

Memory Cards

You can use up a lot of memory when shooting at night, especially if you are shooting large stitched images or taking repeated exposures throughout the night. Fortunately, the capacity of memory cards keeps rising while the prices keep falling. I recommend a 32 or 64 gigabyte card so that you don't have to keep changing cards at night.

Batteries

Night photography involves a lot of long exposures, which can use up battery life much more quickly than shots taken during the day. Batteries also die faster in cold weather, which you'll often encounter when shooting at night. I recommend having a minimum of two fully charged batteries when shooting at night. If you plan to shoot all night long, you'll likely need even more batteries.

It can be useful to have a power outlet in your car to charge your batteries. If your vehicle doesn't have a built-in outlet, you can purchase a power inverter for your cigarette lighter.

Battery Grip

A battery grip allows you to insert a second battery into your camera. This can be useful if you'll be taking repeated exposures throughout the night like you might do when photographing star trails or when photographing a meteor shower. The brand name battery grips from Canon and Nikon are expensive, so I recommend buying one from a third party. I own a Zeikos battery grip for my Nikon D800e, and it works well. I have found that it's more reliable if you adjust your camera settings to use the battery in your camera first and the battery in your camera grip second.

External Battery Pack

If you want even longer battery life, you can connect an external battery pack to the DC plug that comes with many cameras. This does, however, require some technical expertise. Since camera batteries continue to improve, I find a battery back more than sufficient for most of my needs. If it is not too cold out, I can shoot for about eight hours with my Nikon D800e without changing the batteries.

Remote Shutter Release

A remote shutter release (sometimes referred to as a remote switch or shutter release remote control) is very useful for shooting at night. It allows you to take exposures longer than 30 seconds and to automatically take multiple photos in a row. Some remote releases have programmable timers that allow you to set the exact length of the exposure and the exact number of exposures. These releases are known as intervalometers or timer remotes, and they are especially useful for night photography. I recommend owning at least one intervalometer. I also recommend having at least one backup release, whether it be a standard remote shutter release or an intervalometer. Most remote releases aren't overly durable, and I've often had to turn to my backup when one stopped working.

There are also wireless remote releases that allow you to trigger your camera's shutter release from a distance. This can be useful if you are light painting and want to shine your flashlight far away from your camera.

The brand name remote shutter releases from Nikon and Canon are rather expensive. I recommend buying the Neewer brand remote releases, which can be found on Amazon.com. They aren't quite as durable as the brand names, but they have all of the same features and cost about 1/10 as much. A Neewer intervalometer is called a Neewer Digital Timer Remote, and a standard remote shutter release is known as a Neewer Shutter Release Remote Control. Their wireless remote releases are called Neewer Remote

Control 433MHz 16-Channel Wire/Wireless.

You can also find some inexpensive remote shutter releases on eBay. These typically ship from China.

A remote shutter release allowed me to take a very long exposure and capture star trails over Skyline Arch in Arches National Park. Canon EOS 650 film camera, 28mm, f2.8, 3 hours, ISO 100.

If you don't have a remote release or if yours stops working while shooting, you can still capture exposures up to 30 seconds using the manual mode on your camera. This will be long enough for most shots you will take at night. To minimize camera shake when you hit the shutter release button, I recommend using the shortest self-timer setting you have on your camera.

Some Nikon cameras have built-in interval timers. However, this feature will still limit you to exposures of 30 seconds or less. These built-in timers don't always act quite like you would expect, as I'll describe shortly.

Most Canon EOS cameras don't have built-in intervalometers, but you can add one using the free Magic Lantern software, which installs on your memory card. This can be found at http://magiclantern.fm/. Canon also introduced an intervalometer into their new 7D II, so this may become common with Canons.

When using an intervalometer, you'll first need to set your camera to Bulb mode. Most intervalometers have four programmable settings - Delay, Long, Interval, and Frames. I'll discuss each of these in turn. The built-in timers in cameras have similar settings.

Delay

If you set a time for the delay, the camera will wait that long before starting to take any images. You'll usually want this set to zero. You'll only want to set a delay if you don't want to start shooting right away. This might be the case if you are light painting and want a delay so you can shine the flashlight a good distance away from the camera. It could also be useful if you are setting up two cameras at different locations. If it is still too light out to begin shooting when you are setting up the first camera, you can set a delay so that it starts shooting when it is dark and you are off setting up the second camera.

Long

This sets the length of each exposure. I'll discuss proper exposure lengths for different situations later in this book.

Interval

This tells the camera how long to wait between each exposure. You'll usually want this set to one second, which is the shortest interval you can program. It's particularly important to set the interval to one second if you are taking repeated exposures to try and capture star trails, meteors, or lightning.

You might want to program a longer interval if you are taking self-portraits at night. Since you'll have to stay as still as possible during the exposure, this will allow you to rest between each exposure. Another time you might want a longer interval is if you are doing light paintings. This will give you time between each exposure to move to a different position and try light painting from different angles.

If you are using a built-in interval timer on a Nikon camera, the interval time does not refer to the time that elapses between each exposure. Instead, it refers to the exposure length plus the time between each exposure. To achieve a one second pause between each exposure, you'll need to set the interval to a time that is one second longer than the exposure length. But there's a catch. Your camera sometimes lies to you! Standard exposure lengths on a camera are 2, 4, 8, 16, and 32 seconds, but they are listed as 2, 4, 8, 15, and 30 seconds. When you set your camera to take 30-second exposures, it actually takes 32-second exposures. Camera manufactures just round this down to 30 seconds. Likewise, when you set your camera to take 15-second exposures, it actually takes 16-second exposures. If you want a one-second pause between each exposure and your exposure length is set at 30 seconds, you will need to set the interval to 33 seconds. If your exposure length is set at 15 seconds, you'll need to set the interval to 17 seconds. For all other times, including 20 and 25 seconds, you can set the interval to one second longer than the exposure length shown on your camera.

N or Frames

This tells the camera the total number of shots you want to take. If you set this to --, your camera will keep shooting until you press stop on the intervalometer.

Filters

In general, I don't recommend using filters for night

To capture this image, I programmed my intervalometer to take repeated exposures. This helped maximize my chances of capturing lightning bolts in an image. Canon 5D, 70mm, f7.1, 38 seconds, ISO 100.

photography. They will decrease the amount of light that is let into the lens and therefore reduce image quality. However, there are a couple of filters that can potentially be useful.

It should be noted that the Rokinon 14mm and Nikkor 14-24 lenses, which I described earlier, do not accept filters.

Fog Filter

A fog filter attempts to mimic the effects of fog by decreasing contrast and creating a glow around the highlights. It can be beneficial at night because it can create a strong glow around the brighter stars and make them appear larger. This can be especially useful if you want stars in a constellation to appear brighter so that the constellation is more easily identifiable.

A fog filter can cause the foreground to appear blurry in a night photo. You will therefore need to blend two exposures - one of the sky with the fog filter and the other of the foreground without the filter. Blending multiple exposures will be discussed in Chapter IX. This chapter is geared towards more advanced photographers, so I only recommend using this filter if you are comfortable with blending multiple exposures.

Good fog filters for night photography are the Tiffen Double Fog 3 and the Kenko Pro Softon Type-A.

Star Filter

A star filter will create spikes of light around bright lights in an image. The spikes will be larger and more intense around brighter lights. Since most stars are rather faint, the star filter will have minimal effect on them. However, it can produce noticeable spikes around some of the brightest stars and planets. It will have the most visible effect around the moon.

Many star filters are named for the number of spikes they create around the light source. A 4 point star filter will create four spikes, a 6 point filter creates six spikes, and so on. I personally find the 6 point filter to have the most pleasing effect.

Software programs called Star Spikes Pro and Astronomy Tools Actions Set can produce a similar effect to a star filter. However, these programs give you more control over how you want the spikes to appear and are less expensive than most star filters.

If you prefer to use a filter, I recommend the Tiffen Grid Star Effect Filter.

Bubble Level

A bubble level can be a simple but very important tool for a night photographer. Since you often can't see what you're shooting, it can be easy to forget to make sure the camera is level. Many tripod heads have built-in bubble levels, but most of these don't work for shots taken with a vertical orientation. I therefore recommend searching eBay for an inexpensive two-axis bubble level that can be mounted on the hot shoe on top of your camera.

Many newer cameras have a built-in leveling feature, so a bubble level may not be necessary for all cameras. However, this feature can use up some of your camera's battery power. If you do use your camera's leveling feature, I recommend assigning a custom button to it, so you don't have to always scroll through the menu to find it.

Dew Heater

If you're shooting in cold weather, your camera lens can fog up if it is suddenly introduced to cold temperatures. The best way to prevent this is to keep your camera equipment cold by storing it in the trunk of your vehicle rather than in a warm room. You will, however, want to store your batteries in a warm location. Cold batteries do not last as long as warm ones, so this can help maximize battery life. You'll probably need to bring your batteries inside to charge them anyway.

If you can't always keep your camera cold, you can buy a dew heater. This can keep your lens warm and prevent it from fogging up. Dew heaters can, however, be rather expensive. A less expensive, though less efficient solution, is to attach one or more hand warmers to the side of your lens using rubber bands.

Lens Cleaning Cloth

A lens cleaning cloth can be useful for cleaning dust off of your lens. It can also be used to defog a lens.

When I captured this image of the northern lights over Alaska, it was -15° F. In a situation like this, having the right clothing is of paramount importance. Canon 5D II, 20mm, f2.8, 6 seconds, ISO 6400, five images stitched together.

The lens will probably fog up again fairly quickly, so this should only be done if none of the solutions in the previous section are available to you. However, it is better than nothing and should give you time to get some shots before you have to wipe it clean again.

CLOTHING & SURVIVAL GEAR

Photographing in the wilderness at night can be dangerous if you are unprepared. I've provided recommendations on clothing and survival gear that you should consider taking with you. This is just a basic list and is not intended as a thorough guide for all situations. If you haven't spent much time at night in the wilderness, I recommend taking your photos fairly close to your car. There are countless photographic opportunities that don't require hiking.

Clothing

Even if it is warm out during the day, it can get cold at night. Be sure to always check the weather forecast beforehand and dress appropriately.

You should dress in layers, so that you can remove some clothing if you're hiking and start to get hot. You don't want to start sweating, as the sweat can later freeze, making you much colder.

I recommend a base layer consisting of socks, bottom pant, long-sleeve top, and baklava. The fabric I prefer for the base layer is merino wool. Not only is it very warm and comfortable, but it also remains remarkably stink-proof, even if you wear it for many days in a row. You should avoid using cotton as a base layer, as this fabric retains moisture and dries slowly, which can make you very cold.

If it is going to be below 45° F, I recommend having at least two layers of clothing over most of your body. If it is going to be below 10° F, I recommend having at least three layers of clothing covering most of your body. Hand warmers and foot warmers are also very important, as these are parts of your body that are hardest to keep warm.

Some gloves I recommend for photography are Heat Factory Pop-Top Mittens with Glove Liner. The top of these mittens can be folded back, so that you just have a glove over the fingers. The glove is thin enough to allow you to operate your camera. When you're not shooting, you can put the mitten top on to keep your fingers warm. You can also insert a hand warmer into the mitten top. If it's really cold, you can wear a glove liner under this and/or a large mitten over it.

Verseo makes battery-heated ThermoGloves that are thin enough to operate a camera with. One drawback is that the charge only lasts a couple of hours on full power. I've also found that the wires inside

To capture this image of Hickman National Bridge in Capitol Reef National Park, I had to hike at night in rough terrain in a remote area. In a situation like this, having the right survival gear is more important than having the right camera equipment. Canon 5D II, 50mm, f1.8, 30 seconds, ISO 6400, 26 images stitched together.

---

the fingers can easily become misaligned with the glove and pinch your fingers. However, these gloves can be an option if you are shooting in below-zero temperatures where other gloves may not provide adequate warmth. Even with these gloves, I do still recommend hand warmers if it is very cold.

Some boots I recommend are the NEOS overshoes. They can be worn over your normal shoes, which allows you to add an extra layer of warmth. It can be a little cumbersome hiking long distances in these. However, I typically don't venture too far from my car in these circumstances due to the dangers of hiking in frigid cold temperatures at night. I own the Navigator 5 STABILicers, which give great traction when walking on icy surfaces. They also have extendable gaiters, which are good for walking through, or standing in, deep snow.

Food & Water

Always bring plenty of food and water with you, especially if you plan to hike at night. Even if this isn't needed for survival, it can keep you motivated to stay out a little longer to get the shot you want.

Flashlights

If you're photographing alone at night, you should always bring at least two flashlights in case one stops working. A headlamp is very convenient, as it frees your hands up while hiking. Flashlights are also useful if you want to do light painting to illuminate the object you are photographing. I will discuss what flashlights I recommend for this in Chapter VI.

Bright flashlights can significantly disrupt your night vision. It takes about 10 minutes for your cones to adapt to the dark and over 30 minutes for your rods to adapt. Anytime you shine a bright flashlight, you will lose most of your night vision and your eyes will take the same amount of time to readapt. Some flashlights have red lights that are supposed to help preserve night vision. The reason behind this is that the rods we use to see at night are less sensitive to red light, so these flashlights should not disrupt our night vision as much as other lights. However, for somewhat complex reasons, this is largely a myth. Deep red lights can be beneficial at very low levels, but red lights can actually be more harmful than helpful at brighter levels.

The biggest factor for preserving night vision is not the color of the light but how bright it is and how long you use it. If you want a flashlight for night vision, I recommend the Proton Pro, which has both red and white lights and is dimmable to very low levels (approximately 0.3 lumens). This flashlight also has an automatic SOS mode and is very small and lightweight. One problem with this light is that you may also need to carry a headlamp for hiking and a third flashlight for light painting, as it is not as useful for these applications.

Personally, I find the Coast HL7 Focusing 196 Lumen LED Headlamp, which I describe in more detail in Chapter VI, suitable for preserving some night vision. It is dimmable down to three lumens and can be increased to 196 lumens when you are hiking. Also, it is focusable and can throw out a wide beam for light painting. I do, however, carry a second flashlight that I use for most of my light painting and as a back-up when hiking.

I've gone into some detail about preserving night vision, as I know it is very important to some photographers. Personally, though, I don't find preserving night vision to be all that important for photography. The camera can pick up far more detail and color than our eyes, regardless of how long they have had to adapt to the dark. You will need to learn how the camera will "see" at night and how images will look when photographing different parts of the sky. You simply can't get an adequate feel for this by viewing the scene with your eyes.

Survival Kit

You can create your own survival kit or buy one that comes prepackaged with many different items. Some things you should include in a survival kit are a fire starter, first aid supplies, a survival blanket, and a multipurpose tool or knife.

Map, Compass, & GPS Unit

Navigational tools are essential if you plan to hike at night. It's much easier to get disoriented at night than it is during the day. I recommend hiking to a location while it is still light out, so you can become familiar with the route for the hike out in the dark.

Personal Locator Beacon

A personal locator beacon can transmit your location to a satellite in order to alert rescue crews. One of the more popular beacons is the SPOT Satellite GPS Messenger. With this device, friends and family are able to track your location in real time and you are able to send them alerts to let them know you are okay. This beacon currently retails for $170, but it also requires a service plan starting at $10/month.

If you don't want to pay a monthly service plan, you can purchase the Fast Find Personal Locator Beacon. This unit costs a bit more than the SPOT, but you'll save quite a bit in the long run with no monthly fees. It can only be used in an emergency and can't be used to let friends and family know you are okay.

Sleeping Bag and/or Ground Mat

A sleeping bag or ground mat can come in handy if you are doing long exposures or repeated exposures in an attempt to capture star trails or meteors. You can lie back and relax while the camera does all the work!

II. Planning Your Shots

If you take the time to plan when it will be best to photograph at a particular location at night, you will almost always get results that are superior to an unplanned shoot.

There are many things you need to consider before you ever leave your house. Do you want the Milky Way in the photograph? Do you want the foreground illuminated by the moon, or do you prefer to shoot the scene under no moon? Do you want to try to capture meteors in your image? Do you want specific planets or constellations in the image? Do you want any clouds in the sky?

By planning your shot in advance, you can gain much more control over the appearance of the final image. I'll discuss many of the things you can do to previsualize your photographs in this chapter.

SOFTWARE PROGRAMS

There are many computer software programs that can help you plan a photo shoot. I'll describe some of my favorites below. The great thing about these programs is that all of them are free!

Stellarium

Stellarium is a remarkable software program that shows exactly how the night sky will appear from any location around the world at any date and time you choose. This program can be downloaded at http://www.stellarium.org/. It can also be purchased as an iTunes or Android app for a small fee.

When you open Stellarium, the first thing you should do is select a location close to where you will be photographing. You can do this by pressing F6. A dialog box will appear that will give you hundreds of locations around the world to choose from. Choose a medium to large city that is closest to the spot you will be photographing. Alternatively, you can enter the exact GPS coordinates where you plan to photograph and add that location to the list.

You will next want to change the time and date to see how the night sky will look at different times. You can do this by moving the mouse to the bottom left of the screen until a menu pops up. On the very right side of the menu, you will see buttons that look like the Play, Fast Forward, and Reverse buttons on a DVD player. Click on these buttons to "fast forward" in time, "reverse" back in time, or hit the Play button to simply move forward in real time. Alternatively, you can press F5 and enter an exact time and date.

Stellarium shows the location of the moon and the planets, which is very helpful as these objects constantly change position in the sky relative to the stars.

Stellarium is also very useful for previsualizing the Milky Way. The Milky Way is one of the most dramatic objects to photograph in the sky, and its location changes constantly throughout the night and throughout the year. By checking Stellarium to see where the Milky Way will be in the sky, you can plan for it to be over a specific object, like a rock formation or a mountain.

You can increase the brightness of the Milky Way to help previsualize it better. Press F4 to open the Sky panel, and under Stars you can adjust the Milky Way Brightness setting. There's also an option on the next panel down under Atmosphere that allows you to simulate light pollution. This can be useful if you can't get to a really dark area. Stellarium uses the Bortle Dark Sky Scale, in which 1 represents a very dark sky and 9 represents an inner-city sky.

Left: By planning to shoot when there was a quarter moon behind and to the left of me, I was confident that West Mitten in Monument Valley would be well-lit during the long exposure I used to capture star trails. Canon EOS 650 film camera, 24mm, f4.0, 2 hours, ISO 100.

I also recommend clicking on the Scale Moon option under Planets and Satellites. This will make it easier to spot the moon, and it will show the moon phase.

The Photographer's Ephemeris

Although Stellarium is my favorite program to use for previsualizing the night sky, I also find The Photographer's Ephemeris (TPE) to be a valuable tool. This program can be found at http://www.photoephemeris.com/ or purchased as an iTunes or Android app.

TPE shows the moon phase for any given day and also shows the times of moonrise, moonset, sunrise, and sunset. It shows the exact direction in the sky from which the moon and sun will rise and set. Although this information can be gleaned from Stellarium, it is easier get from TPE, as it is the primary purpose of this software. TPE also has a built-in map, so you can figure out what direction you will be shooting at any particular location. This can be useful if you want to know where the moon will be relative to the direction you will be photographing (like the photo on page 26).

Google Earth

Most photographers are probably familiar with Google Earth, which can be downloaded at http://www.google.com/earth/. It is also available for free as an iTunes or Android app. This is an incredibly detailed mapping software that can help you find places to photograph. You can use the ground-level view in Google Earth to get an idea of what the terrain looks like. You can also view photos that other people have uploaded to Google Earth to get a better idea of what certain places look like.

If you go to View > Sun, it will show you how the sunlight will alter the light and shadows on the land throughout the day. Even better, it will show how the stars will appear over any location on Earth at

night. It doesn't have as many features as Stellarium for viewing the night sky, but it is a great way to preview how both the foreground and sky will look at ground level for any photo you want to take.

WEBSITES

There are many different websites you can use to plan your shots. I'll describe some that I frequently use.

Weather Sites

You will need to shoot under clear skies or partly-clear skies in order to capture any stars in your image. I therefore recommend checking the weather forecast before heading out on a photo shoot.

Since there are a lot of weather sites to choose from, I decided to look for scientific surveys that compared various sites. I found two older surveys that compared the forecasts to the actual recorded temperatures. For night photographers, it's more important that the forecast be accurate for cloud cover. However, I assumed that if a site was reliable at predicting temperature, it would likely be reliable for predicting cloud cover as well.

A 2007 study by Brandon U. Hanson found Weather.com and Intellicast to be the most accurate sites. A 2003 study by Eric Floehr found MyForecast and AccuWeather to be the most accurate. The sites

I previsualized this image of East Pawnee Butte in Pawnee National Grasslands using Stellarium. This photo was taken on June 25, 2011 at approximately 10:30 p.m. If you go to this time and date on Stellarium, select Greeley, United States as your location, and look to the east, you will see that the Milky Way looks very similar to how it looks here. Canon 5D II, 50mm, f1.6, 10 seconds, ISO 6400, 86 images stitched together.

that focused strictly on weather all did fairly well. The only sites that did poorly were news sites like BBC and MSN that do not focus solely on weather. One exception to this is local news sites. Their regional forecasts can often be more accurate than national weather sites, since they are very familiar with weather patterns in that area. Local news sites, however, were not included in these surveys.

Since there is no clear consensus as to what sites are best, I think that most any weather site will work well. If there's a site you already use and are familiar with, that may be your best option. Or, you might consider Weather Underground (which I'll describe shortly), due to the large number of features it has for astronomy and for predicting cloud cover.

If you're able to leave on short notice or have flexibility in where you're traveling, the extended forecasts on weather sites can be useful. These forecasts aren't overly reliable if it will be partly cloudy or mostly cloudy during that time, as clouds are notoriously unpredictable. But if there's a forecast for nothing but clear skies for ten days, you can be pretty confident that it will be a good time for night photography.

Most sites will also have short-term hourly forecasts that can give you an idea of how much cloud cover there will be over the course of the night. If the weather forecast calls for it to be mostly cloudy throughout the night, you probably won't have much luck. I usually stay home on nights like these. If the forecast calls for it to be partly cloudy, you might have more success, as you can get some dramatic shots if you're able to get both the stars and clouds in an image.

Weather Underground

WeatherUnderground.com was not included in one of the above surveys and finished in the middle of

The forecast called for it to be partly cloudy at the beginning of the night and turn to mostly cloudy later. I took a chance that I could get some stars over Moses and Zeus in Canyonlands National Park, along with the clouds. Since the clouds weren't moving very fast, I used a six minute exposure to get them to appear blurred. This resulted in the short star trails you see here. Nikon D800e, 35mm, f1.4, 352 seconds, ISO 100.

the pack on the other one. However, this site has a lot of useful information for night photographers.

You can view weather maps by clicking on Maps and Radar and selecting Current Conditions Maps. The map called Satellite under the Cloud Cover Maps will show you detailed maps of the current cloud cover throughout most of the planet. If you click on Forecast & Models near the top of this page and then click on Sky Cover, you will see a map with a rough estimate of how the cloud cover is expected to change over the next six days.

These maps are useful if it is expected to be overcast in your area, but you are intent on getting to a location to shoot a celestial event, like a meteor shower or an eclipse. If you find an area you can drive to that is expected to have clear skies, you can give yourself a chance of getting the shot you want.

You can also view cloud cover predictions if you search for a specific town and click on Table under the 10-Day Weather Forecast. On the right side of the table, it will show you an hourly forecast of the percentage of cloud cover that is expected.

This website also has an astronomy section near the bottom of each town's forecast page. This section tells the twilight times, as well as the moon phase and the times of moonrise and moonset.

Weather Underground has free Android and iTunes apps.

ClearDarkSky.com

ClearDarkSky.com is used by astronomers to determine when it will be best to observe stars at night. It has forecasts for many locations throughout North America. I've sometimes found it to be more accurate than most weather sites at forecasting exactly when the skies will clear up. Other times, the forecasts have been way off, probably because it's not updated as frequently as other sites. So I recommend using it in conjunction with another weather site. ClearDarkSky.com only forecasts two days out, so it is not useful for long trip planning.

To use ClearDarkSky.com, click on a U.S. state and then look for a town close to where you will be photographing. In the charts they provide for each town, the most important thing for photographers to look at is Cloud Cover. If the squares under any of the hours are white, it means you can expect overcast skies during that hour. If they are dark blue you can expect clear skies, and if they are light blue you can expect partly cloudy skies. If you click on any of these squares, it will show you a map of the expected cloud cover at that time.

There is additional information available on these charts, such as Transparency and Seeing. These charts are useful for discovering just how clear the skies will be at night. However, they are more useful for astronomers trying to observe far distant objects that require ideal viewing conditions. For photographers, as long as there are few clouds and you are away from light pollution, you should be able to capture great images regardless of these other conditions.

The information found on ClearDarkSky.com is also available in an app for iTunes called myCSC and an Android app called Clear Sky Droid.

Light Pollution Atlas

If you are photographing at night near a city or town, light pollution can be a major issue. It can drown out light from the stars, making them more difficult to see and photograph. It can also give a murky color cast to objects you are photographing, and it can create an unnatural glow in the sky. Although I discuss techniques for minimizing the effects of light pollution in post-processing in Chapter X, your best bet is always to get far away from cities and towns. You can see a map of light pollution levels throughout the world at http://djlorenz.github.io/astronomy/lp2006/. Click on View Atlas in Google Maps to view the map in much more detail.

Ideally, you'll want to shoot in locations that aren't colored in the map. Unfortunately, the eastern United States and western Europe have few such locations. If you are shooting in these areas, you should at least try to get to a location that is shaded purple or green.

While this map is very useful, it is a little outdated. You can find a more recent map at http://www.blue-marble.de/nightlights/. This map is not color coded, so it is not quite as easy to use.

There's also an iTunes app called Dark Sky Finder and an Android app called Loss of the Night that provide similar information.

Astronomy Calendar

Seasky.org has an astronomy calendar that lists most of the major celestial events that occur over the course of the year. It includes dates of major meteor showers, eclipses, planetary conjunctions, and more. The calendar can be seen at http://www.seasky.org/astronomy/astronomy-calendar-current.html.

Starry Nights Wall Calendar

I now produce a wall calendar that features my night photos and provides dates of many celestial events that you may want to photograph. This calendar can be found at http://www.collierpublishing.com.

ITUNES APPS

In addition to the ones I've already mentioned, there are a large number of applications made just for iTunes that can help you plan your night shots. I won't overwhelm you with information on all of these apps, as there is now one app that does practically everything you'll need to plan your night photography.

PhotoPills

This is an amazingly comprehensive program. It has a Planner screen similar to The Photographer's Ephemeris that shows you where and when the sun and moon will set and rise each day. However, it goes beyond what TPE is capable of. You can enter where you want the moon to be, and it will calculate the exact dates and times when it will be in that position. It also has a 3D Augmented Reality Viewer. This allows you to point your iPhone or iPad at a subject, and it will show exactly where different celestial objects will appear in the scene at different times of the night, including the moon and the Milky Way.

PhotoPills lets you keep track of all the places you want to photograph by saving them as Points of Interest. Plus, it has a depth of field calculator that will tell you the hyperfocal distance and the nearest and farthest distances that will be in focus with different camera settings. It also has a long exposure calculator that can help determine the proper camera settings for very long exposures.

This app is even useful for shooting star trails. The Star Trail Stimulator allows you to see how star trails will appear when facing different directions and with different exposure times.

There are many other useful features on PhotoPills that you can learn about by watching the tutorials on their website at http://www.photopills.com/

Triggertrap

This free app works like an intervalometer and lets you set your camera to take repeated long exposures. You do have to connect your mobile device to your camera with a short cable.

ANDROID APPS

Sky Safari

This program is also available on iTunes, but I find PhotoPills more useful for photographers. Since PhotoPills isn't available for Android, this app is a great alternative. Like PhotoPills, you can point your phone up, and it will give a real-time view of objects in the sky. You can also move forward in time to see how the sky will change at night.

Photo Tools

This is a free app that can do some of the same calculations as PhotoPills, including determining depth of field and long exposure settings.

DSLR Remote

Although Triggertrap is also available as an Android app, DSLR Remote may be a more useful alternative to an intervalometer. With this free app, you can control your camera from a distance via infrared, as long as your camera has an infrared receiver.

I shot this image of rock formations in Escalante National Monument under no moon so that I could capture more detail in the stars and the Milky Way. I decided that the shapes of the rocks were interesting enough to work as silhouettes and that they didn't need to be illuminated by the moon or by a flashlight. Canon 5D II, 14mm, f2.8, 30 seconds, ISO 6400.

MOON PHASES

Knowing what the current moon phase is and where in the sky the moon will be is very important for night photography. Shooting under a full moon can produce drastically different results than shooting under no moon. While there is no right moon phase to shoot under, there are distinct advantages and disadvantages to shooting under different phases.

No Moon

The biggest advantage of shooting under no moon is that your camera can capture more stars, since moonlight obscures fainter stars. This is particularly important if you want to capture dramatic shots of the Milky Way.

The biggest disadvantage of shooting under no moon is that less light enters your camera and there will be more noise visible in the photographs. The noise can be minimized by using the proper equipment and/or stitching images. However, all other things being equal, a photograph shot under a full moon will have less noise than a photograph shot under no moon.

Photographs taken under no moon and with no light painting will usually render foreground objects as dark silhouettes. This can be good for objects with interesting shapes, like a saguaro cactus or some of the bizarre rock formations in America's Desert Southwest. It probably won't work as well for things with less distinct shapes, like mountains or canyons.

Deciding whether you want to shoot under no moon is ultimately an artistic decision. I often prefer shooting under no moon because of the dramatic starscapes I can capture with no moonlight obscuring the view. Also, I think that silhouettes can emphasize how dark it is and keep the primary focus on the dramatic night sky.

If you want to do any light painting, you'll generally want to do this under no moon. You can capture the dramatic dark skies, while illuminating some of the foreground.

Full Moon

The advantages and disadvantages of shooting under a full or gibbous moon are the reverse of shooting under no moon. With the bright light of a full moon, you will get less noise in your images. This can be advantageous if you are using an older digital camera or if you don't have a lens with a wide aperture. For instance, if you are shooting at f4.0, you may get unacceptably noisy images when shooting under no moon. One option is to shoot large stitched images, which will be discussed in Chapter VIII. However, if you're new to night photography, this can be a daunting challenge. So it might be best to plan to shoot under a bright moon until you get more comfortable shooting at night or can invest in some better equipment.

It can also be good to shoot under a full moon if you're forced to shoot in an area that has some light pollution. The light pollution can create unnatural colors in the foreground and in the sky, especially in the clouds. The bright white light of the full moon can drown out some of the light pollution. However, if you are too close to city lights, even the full moon will not help much. In this case, it may just be best to find a darker location to shoot.

Another potential advantage of shooting under a full moon is that it will illuminate the foreground and bring out the color and detail in the scene, in much the same way as the sun would. If the foreground is the most important part of your image and you're not as concerned with capturing a dramatic starscape, you may want to shoot under a full moon.

The biggest disadvantage of shooting under a full moon is that it obscures the light from the stars, and the skies will not look as impressive.

The Anasazi ruin in Hovenweep National Monument was the main focus of this image. I therefore shot under a large gibbous moon to minimize noise and maximize detail. The bright sky from the moon did obscure the stars, though. Canon 5D II, 24mm, f1.6, 20 seconds, ISO 600.

Another disadvantage is that it is difficult to capture long star trails under a full moon, as you can easily overexpose the image. You can get around this by combining multiple exposures on a digital camera, which I will discuss in Chapter VII. However, the star trails will be fainter than if you shot under no moon or a crescent moon.

It's generally best to photograph with the moon behind you, so that it illuminates the front of the object you are photographing. Also, it is usually better

Supapak Mountain near Wiseman, Alaska would have looked like a round, dark blob under no moon. The quarter moon illuminated its jagged edges and bright patches of snow. The moon did not obscure as many stars as it would have if it had been full. It also allowed the northern lights, which were relatively dim on this night, to stand out more. Canon 5D II, 24mm, f2.8, 10 seconds, ISO 6400, nine images stitched together.

to shoot with the moon low in the sky. If it is high in the sky, it can produce harsh light, just like the sun does during the day. Shooting with the moon behind you and low in the sky will also keep the part of the sky you are photographing a little darker and more stars will be visible.

A full moon will be up most of the night. So if you will be facing west when photographing, it's probably best to photograph early in the night when the moon is low in the sky in the east. If you're going to be facing east, it's generally best to photograph early in the morning when the moon is low in the sky in the west.

Crescent Moon

While there can be some advantages to shooting under a full moon, I find that the bright light usually obscures the stars too much. Also, with newer technology and proper exposures, noise is not as big of an issue as it used to be. I therefore find shooting under a crescent moon preferable if I want to render detail in the foreground and capture more stars in the sky.

An interesting fact about the quarter moon (or a 50% illuminated moon) is that it is only 9% as bright as a full moon. This is surprising to many people who would expect a quarter moon to be half as bright as a full moon. However, light from the sun bounces directly off of a full moon and straight back to Earth. Light from a quarter moon has to bounce at a 90-degree angle to reach Earth, and much of that light is blocked by irregularities on the moon's surface like craters and boulders. The light from a quarter moon therefore obscures the stars much less than a full moon and will often result in more dramatic images.

I generally like shooting under an even fainter moon, when it is 10%-35% illuminated. This provides just enough light to illuminate the foreground, while only somewhat obscuring the stars. A moon that is 10% illuminated is less than 2% as bright as a full moon. However, even this much light is usually enough to illuminate the foreground if you're using good equipment that doesn't produce too much noise. You do, however, need to make sure the moon is directly illuminating the front of the foreground objects, as any large shadows will usually be too dark to render detail under such a dim moon.

If the moon is more than 50% illuminated, I find that it starts to drown out the light from the stars too much. I therefore usually plan my photography trips so that they end after the first quarter moon.

The waxing moon that occurs shortly after the new moon will appear in the western part of the sky after sunset. Thus, it is generally best to shoot under this moon when facing in an easterly direction.

The waning moon that occurs right before the new moon will appear in the eastern part of the sky before sunrise. It is generally best to shoot under this moon when facing in a westerly direction.

Throughout the year, the moon can also move from far south in the sky to far north. It wanders farther north and south than the sun does. You can plan to shoot in a southerly direction when the moon is to the north and in a northerly direction when the moon is to the south.

One exception to this is if you want to include the moon itself in the shot. In this case, you will of course want the moon in the same part of the sky that you are photographing.

MONTHS OF THE YEAR

The time of the year that you photograph is also very important for night photography. Different constellations and different parts of the Milky Way will be visible during different months of the year.

The information provided below is for shooting in the northern hemisphere, since that is where most readers will be photographing. Different constellations will be visible from the southern hemisphere, and you will see different parts of the Milky Way.

The night sky may actually be more dramatic in the southern hemisphere. Two spectacular galaxies, known as the Large and Small Magellanic Clouds, can be seen in the southern skies. Also, the brightest part of the Milky Way rises high in the sky throughout much of the year. In the northern hemisphere, the brightest part only rises a little bit above the horizon.

If you do plan to shoot in the southern hemisphere, Stellarium will provide a great preview of what you can expect to see.

December-February

Those looking to capture dramatic shots of the Milky Way may be disappointed during the months of December to February. During these months, the earth is pointing away from the center of the galaxy at night, and you can only see the fainter parts of the Milky Way. It can still be photographed, but the shots won't likely be as dramatic as they are at other times of the year.

There are still plenty of photographic opportunities during the winter months, though. The constellation Orion is usually visible in the southern part of the sky. This is one of the most impressive constellations, and it is made up of some of the brightest stars. Several other very bright stars surround Orion, including Sirius, which is the brightest star in the sky.

The Andromeda Galaxy is also visible near the Milky Way and the constellation Pegasus in the autumn and winter months.

Another great photographic opportunity in winter is the Geminids meteor shower, which peaks in mid-December and is often the best meteor shower of the year.

One benefit to shooting in the winter months is that the sun will set much earlier, especially in the higher latitudes. You can therefore finish shooting at a reasonable hour.

Another advantage of shooting in winter is that your images will have less dark noise when shot in cold temperatures. This is particularly useful for long exposures that result in star trails. Of course, the cold can also be seen as a disadvantage for those not wanting to brave the frigid temperatures.

March-April

The bright, central portion of the Milky Way begins to make its return at night in the months of March and April. It will rise in the southeastern part of the sky shortly before sunrise. When the Milky Way first rises, it will appear as a shallow arc stretching 180 degrees across the sky, from north to south. This can make for some stunning images if you are able to capture the full band of the Milky Way by stitching together multiple images.

This is also an ideal time to capture zodiacal light, which appears as a faint triangular glow pointing up from the horizon. It is most visible far away from city lights about an hour after sunset or before sunrise.

May-June

For those who don't want to get up in the early hours (or stay up all night) to capture dramatic shots of the Milky Way, you can wait until May or June, when it begins to rise earlier in the night. The center of the Milky Way, which is also the brightest part, will appear highest in the sky on the summer solstice, which occurs around June 20 each year.

The sun also sets at its latest time on the summer solstice, so those wishing to photograph the night sky during this time will have to stay up quite late.

July-September

The Perseids meteor shower occurs in mid-August and, along with the Geminids, it is consistently one of the best showers of the year. Other meteor showers can surpass the Perseids in any given year, but these tend to be less reliable.

The center of the Milky Way will be in the southern part of the sky after sunset during these months. The rest of the Milky Way will appear higher in the sky each night, and it will become impossible to capture the shallow arc that is visible in the spring. Instead, the Milky Way will appear to stretch vertically up into the night sky.

September is another good time to photograph zodiacal light.

October-November

The center of the Milky Way will be located in the southwestern part of the sky after sunset in October and November, and it will set shortly after it gets dark. This is a good time to photograph if you want to capture the Milky Way in the western part of the sky without staying up half the night or getting up very early.

TWILIGHT STAGES

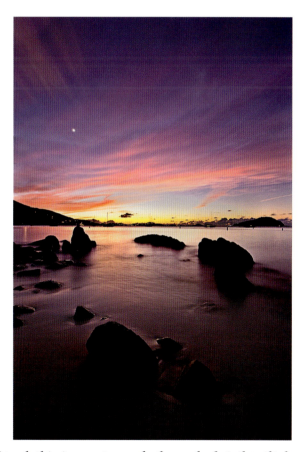

I took this image towards the end of civil twilight on the island of Saint John in the U.S. Virgin Islands. The clouds still had the vibrant glow from sunset, and the planet Venus is visible in the sky. Canon 5D II, 14mm, f8.0, 30 seconds, ISO 100.

It's important to understand the different stages of twilight when photographing at night. There are three stages - civil twilight, nautical twilight, and astronomical twilight. Each of these stages lasts about 30 minutes, though it can be longer or shorter depending on where you are on the planet and what time of year it is. You can determine the exact times each of these twilight stages occurs for your location in the Astronomy section of WeatherUnderground.com. You can also find this information on the PhotoPills iTunes app or on The Photographer's Ephemeris.

I will describe how the sky changes during different stages of twilight. However, the best way to know how images will look during twilight is to take photos throughout each of the stages.

Civil Twilight

In the evening, civil twilight occurs from the time the sun dips below the horizon until it is 6 degrees below the horizon. In the morning, it occurs from the time it is 6 degrees below the horizon until it reaches the horizon. During this time, you can often get vibrant colors in the sky, since a lot of light from the sun is scattered and refracted by the atmosphere. The clouds may have some of the bright orange or pink glow that you would see at sunrise or sunset. You can also capture images of the earth's shadow, which is the shadow that the earth casts on its own atmosphere. This shadow will usually appear with a bright pink band of sky above it known as the Belt of Venus or the anti-twilight arch.

Although I often take shots during civil twilight, I've chosen not to include many in this book. Few celestial objects will be visible during civil twilight, so images taken during this time will look more like daytime shots than night shots. However, you can

The Belt of Venus is visible during civil twilight in this image taken from Arches National Park. Earth's shadow is not visible, as it is blocked by the mountains. Nikon D800e, 300mm, f16, 2.5 seconds, ISO 100.

photograph the moon, Venus, Jupiter, and a few of the brightest stars.

Nautical Twilight

Nautical twilight occurs during the time the sun is 6-12 degrees below the horizon. A lot of the color from civil twilight will have faded, but the stars will still be rather faint. As a result, you may not find many good photographic opportunities during nautical twilight. However, this can be a good time to photograph if your goal is to capture a relatively small number of bright stars in the sky, along with the moon or planets.

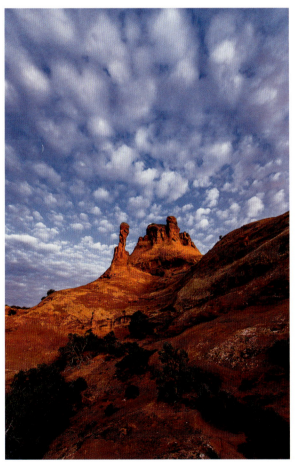

I captured this image at the beginning of nautical twilight. Since I was facing east after sunset, there was still enough light to illuminate the rock formations. There are some faints stars visible in the original file, but most are obscured by clouds. Nikon D800e, 14mm, f2.8, 1.6 seconds, ISO 1200.

You may also want to shoot during nautical twilight if there is no moon out and you want to illuminate a foreground object. If you compose a shot facing east after sunset, there should still be enough ambient light from the west to illuminate the front of the object you are photographing. The stars will be more visible in the darker, eastern part of the sky, especially if you wait until the end of nautical twilight.

Astronomical Twilight

Astronomical twilight occurs during the time that the sun is 12-18 degrees below the horizon. The sky will appear almost completely dark to the human eye, but there will still be some light from the sun refracted through the atmosphere that can be picked up by a camera. The sky will still have a bluish color to it, and there may be some reds or yellows in the direction the sun set (or is about to rise).

Astronomical twilight is one of my favorite times to shoot, and many of the photographs in this book were taken during this time. I find the small amount of color left in the sky desirable for many shots. Also, if there is no moon or a crescent moon, the skies will be sufficiently dark that you will be able to capture many stars and the Milky Way in your images.

TIDES

If you will be photographing by the ocean, it's good to check the tides first, both for photographic purposes and for safety reasons. If you're in an area that can be dangerous at high tide, you'll want to make sure and visit when the tide is low. Also, some compositions may work better during different tides. It's easier to go to a place that you've already photographed during the day, so you know what tides work best for a given shot.

You can find information on the tides online at http://tidesonline.noaa.gov/.

III. Composition

I believe that composition is mainly an artistic decision, and every photographer should strive to develop their own style that sets them apart from other photographers. However, it is still important to understand the factors that can make a good composition. When you take a shot, you can decide which of these factors are most important in the image and which you may choose to ignore. By consciously making decisions about what objects to include in a photograph and how to arrange them, you can begin to develop your style.

SCOUTING

Scouting an area beforehand while it is still light out is perhaps the most important thing you can do to get a good composition at night. It can be very difficult to compose a shot in the dark, especially if you are unfamiliar with an area or new to night photography.

I recommend that you begin scouting a location on the computer, using programs like Google Earth that are described in the previous chapter. Once you've decided on a location, try to arrive at least an hour before sunset to scout the area and look for an optimal composition. This will give you time to walk around and visualize compositions from many different angles until you find one that really works. Always consider both horizontal and vertical compositions, and consider how the shots will look with lenses of different focal lengths.

You may want to take your camera off its tripod and view different compositions through the viewfinder. You can take snapshots from different spots and with different lenses and review them to really get a feel for what composition works best.

Try to previsualize where objects in the sky, especially the Milky Way, will appear after it gets dark. You can do this by checking programs like Stellarium, PhotoPills, or Sky Safari that were described in the previous chapter. If you know the Milky Way will be due south once it gets dark, you can try to find a good composition facing south. If you can't find a composition you like facing south, remember that objects in the sky will move from east to west over the course of the night. So if you find a good composition facing southwest, you can wait for several hours after it gets dark until the Milky Way moves into the southwestern part of the sky.

If you've decided on a good composition before the sun has set, you can set up your camera and set the focus. It is easier to dial in the focus while it is still light out. I recommend doing some test shots at the aperture you plan to use at night to make sure your focus is set properly.

If you are unable to arrive early or if you want to change your composition during the night, you'll need to set up your camera approximately where you want it. You can shine your flashlight on objects in the scene while looking through the viewfinder to get a feel for what will be in your composition. You can then take a test shot and view it on your LCD screen. This will give you a much better feel for your composition, and you can then adjust your camera position until you get it just right.

If it is really windy out, this could affect your composition. The wind can cause the camera to move, resulting in blurred images. Even worse, if you leave your camera while doing long exposures or multiple exposures, the wind could topple the tripod and damage your camera. To make the tripod more stable, you can lower it and spread the legs out wider. Another option is to set up your camera behind a rock formation or other location that is

---

Left: The aurora borealis is spectacular by itself, but including this old, moonlit pier in the composition helped give depth to the image and provide a sense of place. Nikon D800e, 15mm, f2.8, 30 seconds, ISO 1600.

sheltered from the wind. You can also add weight to your tripod by hanging something like your photo backpack off of the center platform or center bar of your tripod.

FOREGROUND SUBJECTS

One of the most important decisions you'll need to make is what to use as your foreground subject. I've seen many night shots where there is just a flat, dark horizon with the night sky above it. While the sky may be dramatic, the shots are little different from countless other images of the night sky. What really sets a good night photo apart from the others is the foreground. Not only does it make the image more unique, but it can also add depth to an image and draw the viewer into the scene.

If you're new to night photography, it's easier to choose foreground subjects that are large and far away, like a mountain or a large rock formation. This can make focusing much easier. You can simply set the focus at infinity and leave it there.

If you're more experienced and want to include closer objects in the foreground, you need to be careful with the focus. You will be shooting with wide apertures at night, which will give you limited depth of field. It can therefore be easy to render part or all of the image out of focus. Always check your focus on your LCD screen after you take a shot. Zoom in on the image and look at the nearest and farthest points in the image and make sure both are in focus.

If you want to include a very close foreground object, it may be impossible to get everything in focus from the nearest point to infinity in a single shot. The solution to this is to take multiple exposures with different focus points and later blend them in post-processing. This is known as focus stacking and will be discussed in more detail in Chapter IX.

I don't recommend focus stacking for those who are newer to night photography. It is easier to start with more distant foregrounds and focus at infinity until you are comfortable with that. Once you are, I recommend gradually including closer foreground subjects until you have it mastered. Using an ultra-wide angle lens, like the Rokinon 14mm, will make this easier, as it provides much more depth of field than a longer lens.

When choosing a foreground, you should also consider whether the moon will be out or not. If there is no moon, your foreground will usually be rendered as a dark silhouette. In this case, you will want to have a foreground that has an interesting shape, like a sandstone rock formation, a gnarled tree, or a saguaro cactus. If your foreground wouldn't make an interesting silhouette or if you want to keep the details and colors in the foreground, you should consider light painting or waiting until the moon will be in the right part of the sky to illuminate the subject.

If the moon is out, you should pay close attention to how the moonlight will affect the foreground. As with the sun, the best light from the moon is usually when it is lower in the sky. However, if you are shooting under a crescent moon that is less than 25% illuminated, you usually won't want the moon to be so low that it is casting long shadows across the scene. Long shadows can work in images taken during the day or even with a brighter moon, as you can still capture some detail in them. However, there is so little light to work with under a thin crescent moon that shadows can appear as black blobs with almost no detail. If you try to bring out detail in post-processing, you will bring out a large amount of noise.

This is not to say that you don't want any shadows when shooting under a sliver of a moon. Small shadows can add depth to an image and bring out texture in foreground objects. You can capture these shadows by shooting with the moon behind you and a little to the left or right. If the moon is too far to the right or left or too low in the sky, it can start to cast longer, undesirable shadows. So you should check to make sure that significant parts of your foreground aren't covered by shadows. If they are, you can wait until the moon moves into a better position and the shadows are diminished. Or, you may have to come back on a different day when the moon is brighter or will be illuminating the foreground more directly. Another option is to try to light paint the dark shadows to bring out some detail in them.

This image depicts Sunset Arch in Escalante National Monument. By knowing where the Milky Way would be as soon as it got dark, I was able to compose the shot and set the focus before the stars came out. I made sure to keep some separation between the Milky Way and the arch. Canon 5D II, 14mm, f2.8, 36 seconds, ISO 6400.

THE NIGHT SKY

You will want to consider how the night sky will appear in your shot when planning a composition. Do you want to capture the Milky Way in your composition? In this case, you will want to consider how the foreground will complement the Milky Way in the image. You'll usually want there to be separation between the foreground and the Milky Way, as opposed to having them overlap. Sometimes, you may have to wait for the Milky Way to move higher or farther west in the sky in order to gain separation with the foreground. Since the Milky Way is so expansive, you'll often want to use a 14mm lens to capture as much of it as possible. Or, you may want to stitch images together to capture an even wider view and a higher-quality image.

Instead of the Milky Way, you may want to capture a specific constellation or star pattern, like Orion or the Big Dipper. In this case, you'll likely want to use a longer lens so that the constellation will appear larger in the shot. You'll probably want to time the shot so that the constellation is low on the horizon and you can include both a foreground subject and the constellation in the image. Longer lenses have less depth of field, so you may need to use focus stacking if you want to include a close foreground object.

There are countless other things you may want to photograph in the night sky, and I'll discuss many of them in Chapter V. With each one, you'll need to consider what lens will work best and how any foreground objects will complement the sky.

Another thing to consider when composing images is clouds. Usually, you will want to photograph when there are no clouds out so you can capture as many stars as possible. However, sometimes clouds can add drama to a scene at night. You will want to photograph clouds when it is partly cloudy and some stars show through in the clear parts of the sky. If it is completely overcast, it can be very difficult to capture good images at night, unless there is a thunderstorm that produces lightning or a moonbow.

If you do shoot when it is partly cloudy, the long exposures will often blur the clouds and show their motion across the sky. The appearance of the clouds will change from shot to shot, and it's difficult to previsualize these images, as our eyes see the clouds as static objects. You probably won't know what you captured until you see it on the LCD screen. Many of the shots may not look too good, but every so often you will capture an image with spectacular clouds. Therefore, the key to capturing good images with clouds is to take a lot of shots in a row and hope that a few of them come out to your liking.

Clouds can also be useful if the moon is bright and obscuring too many of the stars or if it is casting harsh shadows on the scene. If you wait for a cloud to cover the moon, it can diffuse the light and make the image more pleasing.

If you're anywhere near a city, you'll also want to consider light pollution when composing a shot. Occasionally, light pollution can actually help a shot by lighting up clouds or other objects in the photograph or adding some interesting color to the sky. More often than not, though, you'll want to

I captured this image of a ghost building in Mayflower Gulch, Colorado on a summer night under a quarter moon. The clouds in this image added a lot of drama to the scene that wouldn't have been possible on a completely clear night. The distant light on the mountains was cast by the moon peeking out from behind a cloud. Nikon D800e, 14mm, f2.8, 25 seconds, ISO 6400.

My main goal with this composition was to keep it simple. The Milky Way was so spectacular that I didn't want anything distracting from it. I tried to position my camera so that the rock formations roughly aligned with the arc of the Milky Way. I took 50 images of smaller parts of this scene and stitched them together to create a 300 megapixel photo. The red and green colors at the bottom of the sky were produced by airglow. Canon 5D II, 50mm, f1.6, 10 seconds, ISO 5000.

---

avoid light pollution and point the camera away from any city lights. There are ways to minimize or eliminate light pollution in post-processing, which I will discuss in Chapter X. However, the best way to minimize light pollution is to avoid including it in your shot.

PEOPLE & MAN-MADE OBJECTS

While I don't include people or man-made objects in too many of my shots, this is something that can add drama to an image and help tell a story. This can also provide scale in an image.

If you include people in a shot, they will need to stay very still over the course of the exposure or they will appear blurry. It is easier to avoid a blurred photo if you shoot under no moon and render the person as a silhouette. Since the silhouette has little detail, any blurring won't be as noticeable. Alternatively, you can use a strobe light under no moon to illuminate the person. The strobe will put out a quick, bright burst of light, so the person will only need to remain steady at the moment you use the strobe. You'll still need a long exposure to capture the night sky, but as long as there is no other light illuminating the person, any movements they make while the strobe is not on them should not be visible in the final image.

Another option is to blend two exposures - a shorter exposure of the person and the foreground when it is lighter out and a longer exposure of the night sky once it is dark. Techniques for accomplishing this will be described in Chapter IX. This can, however, be a difficult and tedious task, so it is easier to try and capture everything in a single shot.

You will generally want to leave space in the image in whatever direction the person is facing. The viewer's eye will usually be drawn in the direction the person is looking. If there is not much room in this direction, their eye could be drawn right out of the photograph.

Another option for adding the human element to an image is to include a tent in the shot that is illuminated by a flashlight or lantern from the inside.

You'll want to make sure the light from the tent is not overexposing the image. If it is, you'll need to dim the light or blend two different exposures - one for the foreground and the tent and one for the night sky.

Dilapidated cars or buildings can also make for dramatic images. What you decide to include in the shot is really only limited by the imagination.

ARRANGING THE ELEMENTS

Once you've decided what to include in the image, you need to decide how to arrange the objects in your photograph.

Keep it Simple

Although there are exceptions, compositions that are simple and not overly chaotic are generally the most pleasing. This can be especially true at night, when the main element of the image is often the spectacular, star-filled sky. You probably don't want the foreground to be so complicated and busy that it distracts from the sky. Find a primary subject to focus on, and try to exclude anything that doesn't add to the scene.

Check the edges of the frame to make sure there are no extraneous objects in the photograph that should not be there. Part of a tree branch or rock formation at the very edge of the frame might not be easily visible at night, but it can distract the eye away from the primary subject. Generally, it's best to include all of a subject or none of it, rather than having part of it sticking out along the edges. If you do include all of the subject, it's usually best to have a little breathing room between the objects and the very edge of the frame, so that the image doesn't feel too cramped.

Keep it Balanced

If you have strong elements on the left side of the image and no strong elements on the right side, it can cause the image to appear too unbalanced. In this case, you may want to recompose the shot or even change your lens so that the strong elements are more broadly spaced on both sides of the image.

Leading Lines

Leading lines can draw the viewer into the scene and force the eye to follow a predictable path through the image. An example of this is the image on page 40. The converging lines from the wooden pier draw the viewer's eyes from the foreground into more distant parts of the image. Leading lines don't always have to be straight. Curved lines, especially those with the shape of the letter 'S,' can be appealing, as they can lead the viewer's eye on a meandering journey through the scene. Also, strong diagonal lines can give a feeling of movement and add drama to the scene.

It can be difficult to capture leading lines in a night photo, as you'll likely need to include a close foreground subject in the image. Sometimes, you can accomplish this with careful focusing and an ultra-wide angle lens. Other times it will require focus stacking.

Rule of Thirds

I don't believe there are any rules to composition, so I think this would be better referred to as the suggestion of thirds.

If you draw two evenly-spaced vertical lines and two evenly-spaced horizontal lines across an image, the lines will intersect at four different points, as shown in the image on the following page. The rule of thirds states that you should try to have strong elements of a composition located along these lines and, ideally, the strongest elements located at the four points of intersection.

The rule of thirds is based on the notion that we as humans tend to respond better to images that have elements that are not too strongly centered or placed at the very far edge of an image. It tries to strike a balance between these two extremes. This rule is essentially a simplified version of the golden mean. The golden mean describes a geometrical relationship between objects that humans seem to find most aesthetically pleasing. It can be a bit complicated, and even if you understand it, it would be quite difficult to consciously incorporate it into a photograph. So the rule of thirds is an easier way to at least approximate the golden mean.

This image of the northern lights near Fairbanks, Alaska adheres fairly closely to the rule of thirds. The horizon is located a third of the way up and the northern lights take up approximately the top third of the image. The strongest element of the image is located near where the two lines intersect in the upper left. Canon 5D II, 14mm, f2.8, 8 seconds, ISO 6400.

I have seen great images that completely ignore the rule of thirds and have strong central objects or strong elements closer to the edge. So this is a rule that is made to be broken.

Change the Proportions

Most digital SLRs have a 2:3 aspect ratio, meaning that the long edge of the image is always 1.5 times longer than the short edge. However, the scene you are photographing will not always look best with a 2:3 aspect ratio. Sometimes a wide panorama will work better, and other times a square composition will be preferable.

You can crop an image to change the proportions, but you'll want to avoid cropping too much as this will reduce the file size and image quality. It is better to take a stitched image and then crop it as necessary. A wide panoramic photo will be of much higher quality if it is made from five images stitched together than if it is produced from a single image cropped down.

Make Sure Its Level

When setting up your shot, you may be so focused on getting your camera settings right and finding an interesting composition that you forget to make sure your camera is level. Always use a bubble level or your camera's built-in level to make sure that your horizons are horizontal before taking that first image.

IV. Camera Settings

Using the correct camera settings is very important when shooting at night. With the proper exposure, you can capture stunning images with minimal noise and maximum detail. However, a simple mistake can cause a photograph to be very noisy or completely out of focus.

Unlike daytime shots, you can't use automatic settings on your camera when shooting at night. Your camera's light meter will not work in such dark conditions. You will almost always be shooting in manual mode. This chapter is geared toward photographers who already have some understanding of shooting in manual. If you are new to shooting in manual, there are many beginner photography books that can help get you up to speed. Or, you can take a class at a local camera store, community college, or camera club.

APERTURE

When taking photos at night, you will generally want to shoot with the widest possible aperture on your lens. The widest aperture is the lowest number aperture, like f2.8 or f1.8. Wider apertures let more light into the camera. This is very important at night because you need to let in as much light as possible to help minimize noise.

Doubling the number of the aperture from, say, f2.8 to f5.6 will let in only 1/4 as much light. This can effectively make the noise in the image four times worse and is why having fast lenses is so important.

One disadvantage of shooting at such wide apertures is that you will have less depth of field in your shot (meaning that it can be difficult to get both the near foreground and distant background in focus). One solution to this is to not include any really close objects in your foreground. Another solution is to use a very wide lens, like 14mm. Wider lenses allow for more depth of field. In some cases, you may want to use a slightly smaller aperture to get more depth of field, but you should avoid doing this if at all possible. A more advanced option is to use focus stacking, which will be described in Chapter IX.

One exception to using the widest possible aperture is if you have an extremely fast lens, like f1.4 or f1.2. Even with the best lenses, the corners of the image can show a lot of coma at these ultra-wide apertures. The widest aperture I generally shoot with at night is therefore f1.8 or f1.6.

Another instance where you may want to shoot with a smaller aperture is if you're including the moon in your shot and want to capture a sunstar effect with the moon. This will be discussed in more detail in Chapter V.

You may also want to use smaller apertures when capturing star trails. This will be described in Chapter VII.

Other than these exceptions, you will almost always want to shoot at the widest aperture on your lens. This makes selecting the aperture rather easy.

SHUTTER SPEED

Determining the proper shutter speed for shots

Stars rise above Wine Glass Arch in Utah's Canyon Rims Recreation Area. Using the right camera settings was vital in order to ensure I got a sharp image with the stars appearing as round points of light. Nikon D800e, two images blended; exposure for foreground at f6.3, 62mm, 30 seconds, ISO 250 taken shortly after sunset; exposure for sky at f2.8, 62mm, 10 seconds, ISO 6400 during astronomical twilight.

I used the rule of 500 to calculate the exposure time for this shot of sandstone fins in Arches National Park. I used a 24mm lens, so I divided 500 by 24 to calculate an exposure time of 20 seconds. Canon 5D II, 24mm, f1.6, 20 seconds, ISO 3200.

that include the night sky can be tricky. A one-minute exposure will yield better-quality images than a six-second exposure because you are letting more light into the camera and therefore increasing the signal-to-noise ratio. However, during the course of a one-minute exposure the stars will move across the sky and create small star trails in your image. This is not ideal if you are trying to capture stars that appear as round points of light, like you see them with the naked eye.

You need to find a way to get exposures that are as long as possible without producing noticeable star trails. This is where the rule of 500 comes in. With this rule, you take 500 divided by the focal length of your lens to determine the shutter speed. For example, if you are shooting with a 50mm lens, you take 500/50=10. So 10 seconds would be your shutter speed. If you are shooting with a 17mm lens, you take 500/17=29.4. So 30 seconds would be your shutter speed.

If you are not using a full-frame camera, then you will need to first multiply the focal length of your lens by the crop factor before using the rule of 500. For example, if you are using a 16mm lens on a camera with a 1.5 crop factor, you will multiply 16mm x 1.5 to get 24mm as your effective focal length. Then take 500/24=20.8. So 20 seconds would be your shutter speed.

While this is called a "rule," it's really just a suggestion and a good starting point in determining your shutter speed. Once you've become experienced shooting at night, you will get a feel for how different exposure lengths will look with your camera and your intended use of the images. You can then adjust the shutter speed a little to your liking.

You might consider straying from the rule of 500 and using slightly longer exposures in the following circumstances:

- If you are facing due north (or south in the Southern Hemisphere), the stars will move slower and you can get away with a little longer exposure.

- If you don't have the optimal camera and lenses for night photography, you might want to increase exposure time to reduce noise and improve image quality. The longer exposures will produce more elongated stars, but it may be a worthwhile trade-off when shooting with lower-quality equipment.

- When shooting with lenses that are 35mm or longer, the rule of 500 will require shorter exposure times, which will reduce image quality. In this case, it may sometimes be worthwhile to use a slightly longer exposure to get a better quality image.

You might consider using shorter exposures in the following circumstances:

- If you are shooting under a full or gibbous moon, it will be so bright out that you may be able to get away with shorter exposures and still get good quality images. The shorter exposure will allow the stars to appear even less elongated.

- If you are shooting with a very wide lens and you are using good equipment for night photography, you can often use shorter exposures. For example, if you are shooting with a 14mm lens, the rule of 500 states that the shutter speed should be 36 seconds. I usually use a shutter speed of 25-30 seconds in this situation. You can still get good quality images with these exposure times.

The rule of 500 only applies if you want the stars to appear as points of light, not as star trails. The camera settings for shooting star trails will be covered in Chapter VII.

ISO

Once you've determined your aperture and shutter speed, it's time to set the ISO. In the majority of cases, you will want to use the highest native ISO on your camera in order to get the best quality images with the least amount of noise. Native ISOs are represented by a number, such as 3200 or 6400. You should avoid using extended ISOs. These ISOs are generally represented by letters such as H1 or H2. With extended ISOs, the camera software is just manipulating the data that was read from the sensors. It won't improve the

To capture this stitched panorama of the aurora borealis over northern Alaska, I set my camera to its highest native ISO, which was 6400. If the northern lights had been brighter, I would have used a lower ISO to avoid overexposing them. I intentionally overexposed the moon, since it is much too bright to properly expose in a single exposure at night. Canon 5D II, 24mm, f2.8, 10 seconds, ISO 6400, five images stitched together.

image quality, and when shooting with manual settings at night, it could cause the image to be overexposed.

The only time you might want to use extended ISOs is if you are taking a test shot. You can use a very high ISO with a short exposure of a few seconds to get a bright image on your LCD screen. This can quickly give you a good idea of what your composition looks like. However, you should switch back to a native ISO when you are done with your test shot.

It may seem counterintuitive that increasing the ISO will improve image quality. After all, photos taken during the day with high ISOs have a lot more noise than those taken at low ISOs. The reason these images have more noise is because the camera is forced to use a much shorter shutter speed when using high ISOs in order to avoid overexposing the image. With the short shutter speeds, the camera sensors collect fewer photons and the noise competes more strongly with the smaller amount of "real" data.

When shooting at night, you don't need to use a shorter shutter speed when using higher ISOs. This is because it is so dark that you normally won't risk overexposing the image by increasing the ISO. In fact, photos taken with low ISOs at night will probably be vastly underexposed. When you process the image and brighten it to bring out details in the image, you will also be bringing out a large amount of noise that was not as noticeable before.

Images taken with high ISOs will be more properly exposed, and this is the most important fac-

---

To compare image quality at different ISOs, I took test shots at ISOs between 100-6400 with my Nikon D800e. Every shot is underexposed by one stop compared to the one after it. To compensate for this in post-processing, I increased the exposure of each image in Lightroom by one stop compared to the one after it. This allowed me to compare "apples to apples" by making all images equally bright. You can see that the image shot at ISO 100 has a lot of random discoloration and more prominent hot pixels. The image quality successively improves with higher ISOs. There is not much improvement beyond ISO 1600. However, there is a bit of unnatural red discoloration at ISO 1600 that is not present at higher ISOs. Also, the hot pixels are the smallest and least noticeable at ISO 6400.

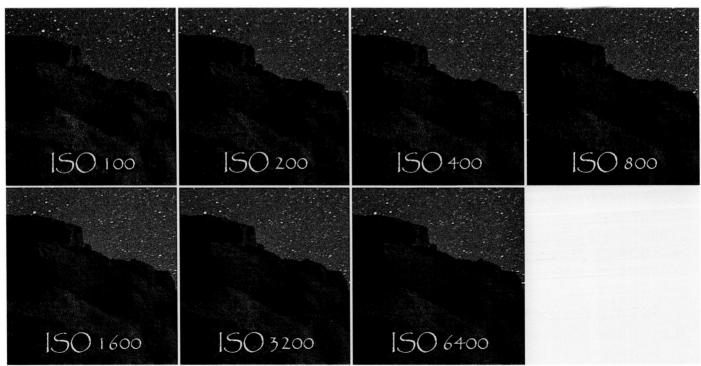

tor in getting a good quality image with as little noise as possible. The scientific reason for this is actually quite complicated. It has to do with how photons of light that hit the sensor are read by the camera, amplified, and then converted into binary numbers that are used to create the image.

One exception to using the highest ISO is if it causes the highlights to be blown out in the image. You can check for this by looking at your histogram. If there is a spike at the very right edge of your histogram, then the highlights are blown out. An image with overexposed highlights will be of noticeably lower quality than an image that is slightly underexposed from the use of lower ISOs at night. So you're better off using lower ISOs if there's any chance of blowing out the highlights.

You need to be especially careful when using high ISOs if you have a camera like the Canon 5D Mark III that has a native ISO of 25600. It can be much easier to overexpose the highlights with such a high ISO. You also won't notice much, if any, improvement in image quality beyond ISO 3200. So you will often be better off using a lower ISO with these cameras.

If there is no moon out or a small crescent moon, it is unlikely that you will blow out the highlights. If there is a full or gibbous moon out, it can be easy to overexpose the image. In this case, simply reduce the ISO until you are not blowing out the highlights. One exception to this is if you are including the moon itself in the shot. It is so bright that you would have to lower the ISO and shutter speed way too much to avoid overexposing the moon. This would significantly reduce the quality of the rest of the image. You're better off letting the moon be overexposed or blending multiple exposures, as will be described later in this book.

Another way you can blow out the highlights is if your shot includes bright sources of light other than the moon, like lava, fire, lightning, or the northern lights. Photographing these light sources is described in detail in the next chapter.

When you use high ISOs at night, it may cause your photos to look way too bright on your camera's LCD screen. However, you should **never** rely on the image on your LCD screen to determine proper exposure. Only rely on the histogram. If the image appears so bright that you're having a difficult time visualizing how the final image will appear, you can change the brightness on your camera's LCD screen to its lowest setting (if it has adjustable brightness). You can also do some test shots with shorter exposures to see a darker version of the image. However, you should not use these test shots. Make sure and increase the exposure length before taking your real shots.

If the image does appear too bright out of the camera, it can be easily darkened later using the Exposure slider in Lightroom or a Levels adjustment in Photoshop. The good thing about darkening images is that it will also make the noise less noticeable in the image.

Even if you use the shutter speed, ISO, and aperture settings described in the previous sections, you may find that your shot still appears underexposed on your histogram. This is not a problem. Sometimes it will just be too dark to get a perfect exposure.

FOCUSING

The easiest way to get a night shot in focus is to set your camera up during the day and get your focus right before it ever gets dark. However, if you can't do this or you need to change your focus during the course of the night, there are many ways to do this.

Focusing at Infinity

If you don't have any near foreground objects in your image, you can simply focus at infinity. The easiest way to focus at infinity is to turn the focus ring on your lens to the infinity marker (∞).

The rock formations in Goblin Valley were about 200 feet away from me, so I was able to focus at infinity. Even if the rock formations had been a little closer, I wouldn't have had to worry about focus as much as normal. Since there was no moon and the rocks were rendered as silhouettes, they had very little detail anyway. It wouldn't have mattered much if they were a bit out of focus. Canon 5D II, 50mm, f1.4, 10 seconds, ISO 6400, 36 images stitched together.

However, this isn't always reliable. On varifocal zoom lenses, the actual spot where infinity is will vary depending on the focal length you have chosen. Parfocal zoom lenses, on the other hand, will not alter the focus as you change the focal length. However, the infinity marker on a parfocal lens or on a fixed focal length lens could be off just a little bit. One exception to this is if your lens has a hard stop at infinity, and the focus ring won't move past infinity. In this case, you should be able to reliably focus at infinity by turning the focus ring until it stops.

If the moon is out and you have an autofocus lens, there is a simple way to focus at infinity. Simply switch your lens to autofocus and center your camera viewfinder on the moon. The autofocus should work on an object as bright as the moon. Just push your shutter release halfway until the focus is locked in on the moon. Then switch your lens to manual focus, and don't change the focus again. Some photographers like to use gaffer tape to tape down their focus ring once it is set to make sure it does not move. I personally don't find this necessary, but if you do this make sure not to accidentally move the focus ring while taping it down.

If the moon is not out or you don't have a lens that supports autofocus, there is another way to focus at infinity, assuming you have Live View on your camera. First, manually set your focus ring near the infinity marker. Next, point your camera towards a bright star in the sky and turn on Live View. In Live View, the LCD screen will appear mostly black, but if you've pointed your camera towards a bright enough star you should be able to see it. Center on this star, and then zoom in as far as you can. The star should now be fairly bright on the screen. Gradually move your focus ring back and forth until the star appears as a small, sharp point of light.

If you have trouble with Live View or you have an older camera that doesn't have Live View, you can start by taking a shot with the focus set at the infinity marker on your lens. Then check your focus by zooming all the way in on the image on your LCD screen. If the image appears out of focus, you should move your focus ring slightly in one direction and take a second image. Now, compare the two photos. If the second photo appears sharper than the first, you can keep moving your focus ring in the same direction until you get the sharpest possible image. If the second photo appears less sharp than the first, you'll need to start moving your focus ring in the opposite direction until you get an image with optimal sharpness.

Since there was no moon out when I shot this image in Arches National Park, I used Live View to focus at infinity. I zoomed in on one of the bright stars and adjusted the focus ring until the star appeared as a small, sharp point of light. Canon 5D II, 24mm, f1.6, 25 seconds, ISO 4000.

If you are using a varifocal zoom lens and you change the focal length of the lens while shooting, you will need to refocus your image before taking more shots. If you don't know if your zoom lens is a varifocal lens, it's best to assume it is and refocus.

Regardless of how you choose to focus your lens, you should always zoom in all the way on your image on your LCD screen to check the focus. It can be very frustrating to spend all night shooting only to find out that later that all of your images were out of focus! Sometimes, if the image is just a little out of focus, it can produce more chromatic aberration around the stars. This will usually appear as an unnatural magenta color around the edges of stars. If you see this, you can adjust your focus slightly until the chromatic aberration is minimized or eliminated.

Focusing Closer Than Infinity

If you have a close foreground subject in your image, you can't simply focus at infinity and take the shot. You'll instead want to focus at twice the distance of the closest object in your photograph. To focus at a precise distance like this, you can simply turn on a flashlight, place it at the distance you want to focus and use autofocus to focus directly on the flashlight. When the focus is locked in, switch back to manual focus to make sure it remains focused at this spot.

Focusing on the flashlight won't work with the Rokinon lenses I described in Chapter I, as they do not support autofocus. In this case, you can again place the flashlight at the spot you want to focus (or simply shine a flashlight on the spot you want to focus on). Then, use Live View on your camera to zoom in and focus on that spot in the same manner I described for focusing on the stars.

Another way to focus if you have an autofocus lens is with a laser pointer. You can shine the laser pointer at the spot where you want to focus and then center your camera on that spot and push your shutter release halfway until the focus is locked. As always when using autofocus at night, immediately switch back to manual focus once you have the focus locked in place.

If none of these options are available to you, you will need to set the focus at approximately twice the distance of the nearest object using the focus ring on your camera.

After you've set the focus using any of the above techniques, you can take a shot and view the image on your LCD screen. Carefully check the image to see if both the nearest and most distant objects are in focus. If only the nearest object is in focus, you'll need to focus a little farther away and take another shot. If only the most distant object is in focus, you'll need to focus a little closer and take another shot. Repeat this until you have an image that is sharp throughout.

If you wind up with an image that has the middle ground in focus, but both the near and distant objects out of focus, it means that you can't get everything in focus with the camera settings that you are using. In this case, you have a few options. You can recompose the image so that the nearest object in the shot is farther away. Or you can switch to a wider lens that has more depth of field. You could also switch to a slightly smaller aperture to get more depth of field. However, you should avoid this if possible, as it will let less light into the camera and result in lower quality images. Instead, I recommend focus stacking, where you take multiple images with different focus points and later blend them in post-processing. This will be described in more detail in Chapter IX.

Understanding Hyperfocal Distance

Up to this point, I've avoided discussing hyperfocal distance, as it can be a difficult concept to grasp if you are not already familiar with it. Understanding hyperfocal distance can allow you to calculate whether everything will be in focus beforehand, rather than using the somewhat ad-hoc approach described in the last section.

In the simplest terms, hyperfocal distance is the closest distance you can focus your camera while still keeping everything at infinity in focus. When you focus your lens at the hyperfocal distance, everything from half that distance to infinity will be in focus. So if you focus at the hyperfocal distance, you will maximize the depth of field in the image. However, this does not leave you with much room for error. If you focus just a little bit in front of the hyperfocal distance, it can render the stars out of focus. Therefore, to give you the most room for error, I still recommend focusing at approximately twice the distance of the nearest object in your photograph. As long your focus point is **farther** than the hyperfocal distance, you can be assured that everything will be in focus.

I shot this image of Faux Falls near Moab using a 24mm lens set at f2.8. The hyperfocal distance was 22.3 feet, which would have allowed me to get everything in focus from 11.1 feet to infinity. However, the nearest object in the image was about seven feet from me, so I wasn't able to get everything in focus with a single exposure. I instead had to focus stack images, which will be explained in Chapter IX. Nikon D800e, 24mm, f2.8, 20 seconds, ISO 3200.

If your focus point is closer than the hyperfocal distance, then you won't be able to get everything in the image in focus using your current camera settings and a single exposure.

If, on the other hand, the nearest object in your photograph is farther away than the hyperfocal distance, you can simply focus at infinity and everything in your image will be in focus. Alternatively, you can still focus at twice the distance of the nearest object. This will give you a little more room for error, but since focusing at infinity is easier, this can be a good option when you don't have a close foreground.

There are many programs and websites that can calculate hyperfocal distance for you if you enter your camera settings. One website that does this is DOF Master at http://www.dofmaster.com/dofjs.html. You can enter different settings to get a feel for how hyperfocal distance changes with different camera settings. It will also tell how the near and far focus points will change. However, this site won't be too useful when you are out in the field. I recommend getting an app for a mobile device that can do this for you. The iTunes app called PhotoPills that I described in Chapter II will do these calculations. For Android users, you can use Photo Tools.

I've provided below some hyperfocal distances for camera settings that are commonly used when shooting at night. These figures are for full-frame digital SLRs. If you don't have a full frame camera, most software programs should allow you to enter your camera model or the crop factor before calculating the hyperfocal distance.

14mm f2.8 - Hyperfocal Distance is 7.6 Feet

If you focus at 7.6 feet, then everything from 3.8 feet to infinity will be in focus.

24mm f1.8 - Hyperfocal Distance is 35.4 Feet

If you focus at 35.4 feet, then everything from 17.7 feet to infinity will be in focus.

35mm f1.8 - Hyperfocal Distance is 75.3 Feet

If you focus at 75.3 feet, then everything from 37.7 feet to infinity will be in focus.

50mm f1.8 - Hyperfocal Distance is 153.6 Feet

If you focus at 153.6 feet, then everything from 76.8 feet to infinity will be in focus.

It is, of course, impossible to focus precisely at 153.6 feet, so you want the nearest object in your image to be a little farther away than 76.8 feet. The above numbers just show the maximum depth of field you can get with these camera settings.

As you can see, ultra-wide angle lenses offer far more depth of field than longer lenses. So if you want a close object in the foreground, you're usually better off using a very wide angle lens.

WHITE BALANCE

Since this scene was illuminated by the moon, I set the white balance to daylight and later lowered it a little in Lightroom. Canon 5D II, 24mm, f1.6, 30 seconds, ISO 4000.

This image shows the northern lights reflected in a pond near Yellowknife, Canada. Since there was no moon out and the image was taken after twilight, I used a white balance of 3800K. Also, it was very cold outside, so I didn't have to worry about reducing dark noise with exposures of just 15 seconds. Nikon D800e, 14mm, f2.8, 15 seconds, ISO 6400.

If you shoot during nautical or astronomical twilight, I recommend setting the white balance on your camera to daylight. If you shoot during civil twilight, you may need to set it to a higher temperature.

If you shoot outside of twilight hours, you'll likely need to use a lower color temperature. If the moon is out, I've found that a color temperature of around 4600K works well. If there is no moon out, you'll likely need to reduce the color temperature to around 3800K to avoid a yellow color cast. In either of these situations, you could use a custom white balance on your camera. This can give you a better idea of how the colors will appear based on the image on your LCD screen.

However, it's probably easier to keep it in daylight mode. As long as you're shooting in RAW, you can always change the white balance settings later. It's easier to fine tune the white balance settings on a computer screen than to try to get it perfect in camera.

NOISE REDUCTION

Most digital SLRs have one or two noise reduction features built into them. Since you're constantly battling noise when taking photos at night, these features may seem very well suited for night photography. Unfortunately, while they can be useful with very long exposures, they're not quite as helpful with shorter exposures.

Long Exposure Noise Reduction

The Long Exposure Noise Reduction feature that is found in most digital SLRs helps reduce dark noise in an image. Dark noise is caused by heat from your camera's circuitry. It may also be referred to as dark current noise or thermal noise.

Dark noise increases in proportion to the length of the exposure. For exposures under one minute at night, the main source of noise is photon noise, not dark noise. Long Exposure Noise Reduction does not target photon noise, so it will usually have only a small impact on noise levels.

When using this feature, your camera has to take a second exposure (known as a dark frame) that takes just as long as the initial exposure. If you're shooting a rapidly changing scene, like one with the northern lights or moving clouds, you don't want to have to wait for the noise reduction after every shot, as you might miss the best shot while waiting. Also, if you are taking repeated exposures to capture star trails, meteors, or lightning, you must have the noise reduction off in order to minimize the time between exposures. The same is true if you're capturing stitched images, as you want to minimize the amount that the stars move between each shot.

The only time I recommend having Long Exposure Noise Reduction on when shooting exposures under one minute is if you are taking single exposures of a slowly-changing scene and you can afford to wait for the camera to take a dark frame after every shot. In this case, it can't hurt to have the noise reduction on, as it can help reduce the noise a little.

Dark noise decreases if you shoot in colder temperatures. So if you are shooting in very cold weather, you probably don't need to worry about it. If, on the other hand, it is warm out and you are able to shoot in shorts and a t-shirt, dark noise can become noticeable even with exposures under one minute. You can benefit more from Long Exposure Noise Reduction in this situation.

If you don't want to wait for the camera to take a dark frame after every shot, you can instead create your own dark frame. Simply put your lens cap and eyepiece cover on (or cover the eyepiece with a cloth or hat) and take a photo. This shot should be taken in similar temperatures and with the same camera settings with which you will be shooting your other photos. If you change your camera settings, you'll need to take a new dark frame. Later, when you choose a photo you like, you can open it and the dark frame in Photoshop. Stack the dark frame on a layer directly on top of the photo. Then, change the blending mode on the layer with the dark frame to Subtract. That's it! Any dark noise captured in the dark frame will be subtracted from the image. Since the dark noise in the two images should be similar, it can help reduce the noise in the image.

Since it is so easy to do, I usually take at least one dark frame while shooting at night. This way I can use the dark frame if the need arises. It's much less time consuming to take a dark frame that can later be applied to any image you take than it is to have the camera take a dark frame after every image.

A disadvantage of taking your own dark frame is that it won't be quite as accurate as the dark frame taken with Long Exposure Noise Reduction. This dark frame will be taken immediately after every shot, and therefore the temperature and conditions in which you take the two shots will be almost identical. However, in most circumstances, it's unlikely you'll notice the difference.

A bigger disadvantage of taking your own dark frame is that it will be less effective at reducing noise if you do too many adjustments to the image in Lightroom or Adobe Camera Raw before applying the dark frame in Photoshop. I recommend only adjusting the white balance and making adjustments to the Highlights or Shadows sliders if it is necessary to recover detail in these areas. Set everything else to zero in Lightroom. You'll need to apply the exact same settings to the dark frame as you do to the image. Then, open the image in Photoshop and apply the dark frame. You can make additional adjustments to the image in Photoshop or, if you prefer, import the image back into Lightroom and continue working on it there.

Long Exposure Noise Reduction can be a lot more effective for very long exposures (5+ minutes), as dark noise increases proportionally with the length of the exposure. However, even when shooting star trails, I rarely recommend doing exposures over five minutes at night with a digital SLR. This is because you can get higher quality images by taking a series of shorter exposures and combining them in Photoshop. If you do this, you can't have Long Exposure Noise Reduction turned on, as the delay will result in gaps in your star trails. You can, however, benefit from shooting a single dark frame. I will discuss this in more detail in Chapter VII.

High ISO Noise Reduction

As mentioned in the last section, photon noise (sometimes referred to as photon shot noise or shot noise) is more problematic than dark noise for exposures under one minute at night. This noise is caused by the random nature in which photos hit the CCDs on your camera sensor.

Some cameras have a noise reduction feature called High ISO Noise Reduction. In newer cameras, this feature targets both photon noise and dark noise. However, it only works on JPEG images. As I'll discuss in the next section, I strongly recommend shooting in RAW, not JPEG. If you are shooting in RAW, this feature will have no effect on your images, so it really doesn't matter

I captured this image on a July night in Utah's Canyon Rims Recreation Area. It was over 70°F on this night, so dark noise became noticeable even with exposures of 25 seconds. The bottom corners of the image had an unnatural red color. I therefore took my own dark frame and was able to minimize the noise in the image. Nikon D800e, 14mm, f2.8, 25 seconds, ISO 3200, focus stacked for increased depth of field.

if it is on or off. If you do shoot in JPEG, I recommend keeping this turned off. The in-camera noise reduction can blur details in your image, which you won't be able to recover later. As I'll discuss in Chapter X, there is computer software called Topaz DeNoise that will do a better job of reducing photon noise in your images than any feature that is built into your camera. This software also does a good job of reducing some dark noise and a third type of noise, known as read noise. Read noise is not very problematic in images taken with newer cameras at high ISOs, so I won't spend much time discussing it.

RAW vs. JPEG

Since you are taking the time to read this book, you are probably serious about getting high quality images at night. I therefore recommend that you always shoot in RAW mode with your digital SLR. When you shoot in JPEG, the camera immediately throws out a lot of the data that is gathered by the sensors. To get the most out of your images, you should begin with as much of this information as possible. The only way to do this is to shoot in RAW.

One reason you want to keep this data is that you will often have very dark shadows when shooting at night. If you shoot in RAW, you can later recover some of the details in the shadows, something that can be difficult or impossible to do when shooting in JPEG.

Conversely, it's possible to blow out details in the brightest parts of the image at night, especially if you're shooting under a bright moon. You can often recover blown highlights when shooting in RAW.

Another important reason to shoot in RAW is that you can later adjust the white balance settings in Lightroom or Adobe Camera Raw. While the daylight setting may work when shooting during twilight or under a moon, it won't often work when shooting under no moon. You could use a custom white balance on your camera, but there is no guarantee that you will get it just right. In this case, you would need to fine-tune the white balance in post-processing, and you can't do this with JPEG images.

The northern lights brightened very quickly while I was shooting in Canada, so I slightly overexposed this image. Since I shot in RAW, I was able to recover most of the blown highlights in Lightroom. Nikon D800e, 14mm, f2.8, 13 seconds, ISO 3200.

If you're not yet comfortable shooting in RAW, you can shoot RAW + JPEG. This will keep the RAW file and also produce a JPEG image. If you do this, I still recommend that you try to work with the RAW files until you're comfortable with them and no longer need the JPEGs.

V. Natural Light Sources

When photographing during the day, the sun will usually be your only source of light. When shooting at night, you can capture many different natural light sources. This can make shooting at night a fascinating process, but it can also make it a lot more challenging. I will discuss most of the natural light sources that you can capture during the night and how to photograph each of them. Some of these light sources, like the moon, reflect sunlight off of them, but several others produce their own light.

THE MOON

The moon will often be used to illuminate the subject you are photographing. However, it is more difficult to include the moon itself in the shot. The easiest way to include the moon in the shot is to shoot it shortly before or after sunrise or sunset. At this time, it is dark enough for the moon to be clearly visible, but it's not so dark that the moon is significantly brighter than everything else. As a result, you can usually capture a shot with a lot of detail in the moon and the landscape with a single exposure. However, these shots look more like daytime images, and you won't get any stars in the photo.

If you wait until it gets dark enough to see the stars, the moon will be so bright that it will overexposed if you try to properly expose the rest of the scene. There are a few options for handling this.

You can let the moon be overexposed and render it as a round white blob in the image, like it is in the photo on page 51. In this scenario, the moon won't look very interesting, but it can still produce a good image if you have other compelling elements in the shot.

Another option is to take two exposures - one short exposure that preserves the detail in the moon and one longer exposure for the rest of the scene. Make sure the short exposure is one second or less; otherwise, the movement of the moon during the exposure can cause it to blur. Also, make sure you are not overexposing the moon in the shorter exposure.

You can blend these two exposures in Photoshop using techniques described in Chapter IX. It can, however, be difficult to achieve a natural-looking blend. In the long exposure, the sky around the moon will be much brighter than in the short exposure. You'll likely need to clone out the moon and the bright area all around the moon in the longer exposure. I only recommend this for those who are very proficient in Photoshop.

It is actually easier to place a short exposure of a moon into a night photo where no moon existed than to place it into a shot where the moon actually existed. This is because you won't have to first clone out the moon from the longer exposure. While I personally would never do this, it is up to each photographer to decide how much artistic license to take with a photo.

A third option is to render the moon as a sunstar, as seen in the picture on the following page. To do this, you need to use a smaller aperture, such as f9.0. This can significantly increase noise, as the lens lets much less light into the camera. However, the moon is bright enough that it can still produce acceptable results. You can use the rule of 500 to determine shutter speed. The moon will have little detail in it, so it doesn't matter if it moves and blurs a little in the image.

If you want to minimize noise and still render the moon as a sunstar, you can take two exposures - one for the moon at around f9.0 and another for the rest of the scene at a much wider aperture, like f2.8. You can then blend them in Photoshop. You'll

---

Left: Lightning strikes peaks of the Sangre de Cristo mountain range, as seen from the Alamosa National Wildlife Refuge. Canon 5D II, 145mm, f5.6, 60 seconds, ISO 100.

probably need to darken the image taken with the wider aperture before adding in the moon from the other exposure. This is a little easier to accomplish than blending a short exposure that preserves detail in the moon, but it still requires some skill in Photoshop.

I took this shot in a remote part of Arizona as the sun was setting. This was an ideal time to capture both the moon and the rock formation in a single exposure. However, it was still so bright out that it can't really be considered a night shot. Canon 5D II, 200mm, f16, 1/6 second, ISO 100.

It is easier to capture a good sunstar effect under a newer moon than it is under a full or gibbous moon. Also, the appearance of the sunstar can differ depending on the lens that you use. So I recommend trying different aperture settings and using the largest aperture that produces an acceptable sunstar.

Another option for achieving a sunstar effect is to use a star filter, as described in Chapter I. This can allow you to shoot at wider apertures and capture images with less noise.

One final option when photographing the moon is to take a very long exposure and capture a moon trail. This technique will be discussed in Chapter VII.

I captured this shot of the quarter moon using an aperture of f9.0. This relatively small aperture produced a sunstar effect on the moon. Canon 5D II, 24mm, f9.0, 25 seconds, ISO 6400.

ECLIPSES

Eclipses are one of the most fascinating celestial events you can witness, and they can produce some spectacular photographs. Solar eclipses only occur during the day, but I'll mention them briefly because they are an astronomical event that night photographers may be interested in.

You can find a list of all upcoming eclipses and the locations where they can be viewed at http://www.timeanddate.com/eclipse/list.html

Lunar Eclipses

A lunar eclipse occurs when the earth passes directly between the sun and the moon at night. During the first part of the eclipse, you'll see just a small part of the earth's shadow covering the moon. If it is a total lunar eclipse, this shadow will grow until it completely blocks the moon. During totality, some light that passes through the earth's atmosphere will be refracted and still hit the moon. This refracted light will have a warm glow to it, and the moon will appear as an orange ball in the sky.

A lunar eclipse is difficult to photograph because

you need to keep your exposures to about one second or less or the moon will move too far during the exposure, causing it to blur. If you want to include any foreground objects in your image, this exposure length will usually not be long enough to capture good quality images of the scene. You'll therefore need to blend two exposures - one short exposure for the moon and a longer exposure for the rest of the scene. This is easier to accomplish than when the moon is not eclipsed. This is because you won't capture nearly as bright of a glow around the moon when it is eclipsed. It will therefore be easier to remove the glow from the longer exposure before adding in the moon from the shorter exposure.

One time when you may be able to capture an eclipse and a foreground object in a single exposure is if the eclipse occurs during civil or even nautical twilight. At this time, there may be enough light on the foreground that you will be able to get good quality shots with the short exposures that are required to photograph the moon.

Another time you can capture an eclipse with a single exposure is if you are using a long telephoto lens and don't include any foreground objects. In this case, I recommend using a remote shutter release and mirror lock-up on your camera. When using a telephoto lens, even the slightest vibration caused by the mirror going up can cause the image to blur. With the mirror lock-up on, the first time you hit the shutter release, it will move the mirror up and the second time you hit it, it will take the shot.

If you want very detailed images of an eclipse, you can use an equatorial mount. This device moves your camera along with the stars and lets you take much longer exposures without blurring the moon. The moon does move relative to the stars, but it moves at a much slower rate than the earth rotates. You can therefore take images of about 30 seconds without getting much blur in the moon or stars.

I shot this image during a total lunar eclipse on December 21, 2010. I used a long telephoto lens to render the moon as large as possible in the image. Canon 5D II, 500mm, f6.7, 1/2 second, ISO 6400.

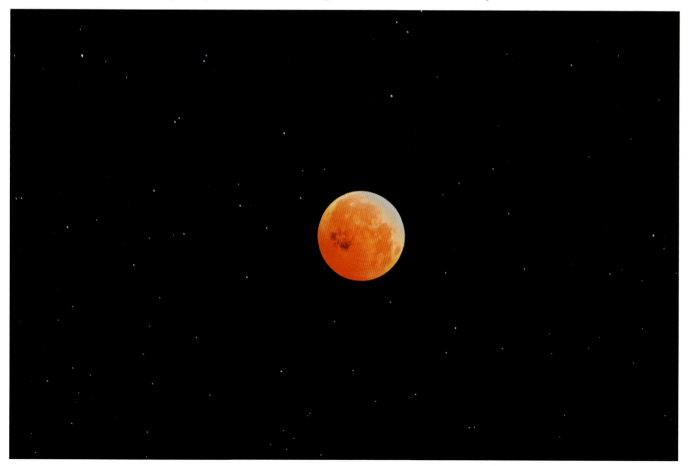

I took this shot of an annular solar eclipse over Cove Arch in Arizona on May 20, 2012. I took two exposures and blended them in Photoshop. Canon 5D II, 200mm, f32, ISO 100 - exposure for the sun was 1/8000 second, exposure for the rest of the scene was 1/60 second.

You can't include foreground objects when using an equatorial mount, as the movement will blur these objects. In this situation, you would again have to blend multiple exposures.

Another option when photographing an eclipse is to take images of many different stages of the eclipse, from the time it just begins to be covered by Earth's shadow until the time it is almost out of Earth's shadow. You can then create a composite image with many different moons at various stages. You can include a foreground object with the moons arcing above it or exclude the foreground and just include the moons in the night sky.

Solar Eclipses

A solar eclipse occurs when the moon passes directly between the earth and the sun, and the moon partially or fully blocks the disk of the sun. If the moon completely blocks the disk of the sun, it is called a total eclipse. If the disk of the moon passes directly in front of the sun, but the disk appears smaller than the sun, it is called an annular eclipse.

Solar eclipses are harder to view than lunar eclipses, as they are visible over a much smaller part of the earth. If there is a total or annular solar eclipse near where you live, it is worthwhile to get out and photograph it, as another eclipse probably won't happen for a long time.

Solar eclipses are more difficult to photograph than lunar eclipses. Even when the moon is covering the disc of the sun, the sun is still extremely bright, especially if it's an annular eclipse. To get a shot with any detail in the eclipse, you'll need to blend two exposures - one very short exposure with a very small aperture and ISO to capture the sun and the moon and one longer exposure for the rest of the scene. You could also use a neutral-density filter or polarizer to diminish the amount of light that is entering the camera.

STARS

Stars will likely be the most common objects you photograph at night. Although stars do move relative to each other, this movement is so gradual that it can take thousands of years for us to notice it here on Earth. Stars therefore appear to us as fixed objects in the sky. The moon and the planets are constantly moving relative to the stars.

Since stars appear as fixed objects, their location is very predictable. Every month, a given star will rise two hours earlier than it did the previous month. After a full year, that star will appear in the same spot in the sky as it did at that time the previous year.

The densest concentration of stars can be found in the band of the Milky Way. Earth is located on a spiral arm far out from the center of the Milky Way Galaxy. As a result, when we look towards the center of the Milky Way, it appears much brighter. When we look away from the center, it appears quite faint.

As discussed in Chapter II, you can use Stellarium to see exactly how the Milky Way will appear at any time and any location on Earth. Since the Milky Way stretches across the entire sky, you'll need to use a very wide angle lens or create a stitched image

I captured this image towards the beginning of astronomical twilight on a night when Jupiter, Venus, and the moon (seen from top to bottom) had all aligned in the same part of the sky. I used a small aperture of f10 to render the moon as a sunstar. Canon 5D II, 24mm, f10, 25 seconds, ISO 6400.

to capture more than a fragment of it.

Constellations can also be fascinating objects to photograph. The two most impressive constellations seen in the northern hemisphere are probably Ursa Major and Orion. The Bigger Dipper makes up part of Ursa Major and is more easily recognizable than the full constellation. It is visible year-round in the northern part of the sky. Orion is visible in the winter months in the southern part of the sky. Sirius, which is the brightest star in the night sky, is visible down and to the left of Orion.

The camera can capture many more stars than the eye can see. As a result, constellations that are clearly visible to the naked eye can get lost amongst all of the other stars in a photograph. I will discuss ways to make the constellations stand out more in the section of Chapter IX called Enlarging Star Size and in the section of Chapter X called Boosting Star Size & Brightness.

PLANETS

From our vantage point, the brightest planets in the night sky outshine any of the stars. Of all the planets, Venus appears the brightest. It is often referred to as the Morning Star because its orbit is inside the earth and it always appears in the sky near the sun. It can therefore only be seen when the sun is not too far below the horizon, either in the morning before sunrise or in the evening after sunset.

Jupiter is the second brightest planet. Since its orbit is outside of Earth's, it won't always be in the same part of the sky as the sun and can appear at any time of the night. Other planets that are bright and readily seen with the naked eye are Mars and Saturn. Mercury is also visible with the naked eye, but it is so close to the sun that it is usually obscured by the sun's light.

A good time to photograph planets is during a conjunction, when two or more of them appear close to each other in the night sky. You can find dates for planetary conjunctions at http://www.go-astronomy.com/solar-system/planets-conjunctions.htm.

Another good photographic opportunity is when the moon is in the same part of the sky as a planet. You can see a list of conjunctions of the planets with the moon at http://astroclub.tau.ac.il/ephem/LunarOcc/PlanetsConj/. You can ignore the dates for Neptune and Uranus. These distant planets will be fainter than many stars, so an image of them will not stand out.

If you're able to capture two or more planets near the moon, this can be an ideal scenario. This is a somewhat rare occurrence. You can determine when this will occur in the link above. If two different planets will be in conjunction with the moon within one or two days of each other, you'll likely be able to capture all of them in a single image.

METEORS

Meteor showers create one of the most impressive displays in the night sky. They are produced when the earth passes through dust particles left behind by a comet or asteroid. When the dust particles hit the atmosphere at great speeds, they burn up and briefly produce spectacular fireballs in the sky.

Meteor showers are predictable and usually occur at the same time each year. A list of meteor showers can be found at http://stardate.org/nightsky/meteors/.

The Perseids and Geminids are typically the most reliable meteor showers each year. The Quadrantids in early January can also put on a good show, but the peak of this shower usually only lasts a few hours. Other meteor showers may run in cycles and be incredible one year and uneventful for several years after that. For example, the Leonids are unspectacular most years, but they reach their peak every 33 years. In 1966, the Leonids produced a mesmerizing display in the night sky, reaching a peak rate that was estimated at over 100,000 meteors per hour! The next peak for the Leonids will not occur until 2032.

If the moon is out, it can obscure the meteors and make them even more difficult to photograph. I therefore recommend shooting meteors when there is no moon out or under a moon that is less than 20% illuminated. If there is a moon out that is

A meteor streaks above Landscape Arch in Arches National Park. I took repeated exposures of this scene in order to capture this meteor. Canon 5D, 24mm, f1.6, 25 seconds, ISO 1600.

---

greater than 20% illuminated, you can wait for it to set or shoot before it rises. If the moon is full or nearly-full, it will be up most of the night, so you will likely be out of luck.

Meteor showers tend to be most active in the early hours before sunrise. However, if you're able to photograph all night long, this will increase your chances of capturing a lot of meteors.

All meteors in a shower will originate from a specific area of the sky, which is known as the radiant. The meteors will not necessarily appear in this part of the sky, but they will all point back towards the radiant. Meteor showers are almost always named after the constellation where their radiant is located. If you locate this constellation in the sky, you'll know where all meteors will radiate from.

You don't necessarily want to point your camera directly towards the radiant of the meteor shower. The meteors you capture near the radiant will generally be moving towards you and will therefore appear shorter. If you point your camera about 90 degrees away from the radiant, you will be more likely to capture longer meteor trails.

Since meteors travel quickly across the sky, they need to be very bright in order to capture them in a photograph. To maximize your chances of capturing a bright meteor in an image, you should take repeated exposures throughout the night and hope that a bright meteor passes through the shot during one or more of the exposures. Unless your camera has a built-in interval timer, this will require a remote shutter release or intervalometer. It may also require extra batteries, as even the best batteries will die within 2-5 hours. If you purchase a battery grip, you can add a second battery to your camera.

The camera settings you need to use are similar to what you would use for a typical night shot, as detailed in Chapter IV. However, I recommend using an ISO of 1600. Some of the meteors can be bright enough that you can overexpose them with higher ISOs. They will still look good if they are overexposed. However, you can sometimes capture color in them if you avoid overexposing them.

I recommend using a very wide angle lens, like

14mm, so that you are able to shoot a large portion of the sky. If the composition you've decided on works better with a little longer lens, this is okay too. You won't be able to capture as much of the sky in your shot, but the meteors you do capture will appear larger and you'll be able to capture fainter meteors. The one problem with this is that the largest meteors may travel all the way across your frame, and you'll only be able to capture a portion of them. Although these large fireballs are somewhat rare, they are usually the most dramatic meteors.

If you do catch a streak of light in your image, it is important to know if it is actually a meteor. There are a lot of things that can produce streaks of light and not all of them are meteors! Airplanes will produce streaks of light, but these streaks will usually be dotted, since the airplane's lights are flashing. Satellites can also produce streaks of light. Many satellites look like straight lines with uniform brightness. However, some satellites produce iridium flares when light is reflected off a highly reflective aluminum antenna. The satellite will get temporarily brighter and fade again, resulting in a non-uniform brightness across the streak of light. Since meteors usually have a non-uniform brightness, it can be difficult to distinguish between a meteor and an iridium flare.

One way to distinguish between the two is to see if the streak of light is pointing back towards the radiant of the meteor shower. This isn't always reliable, however, as a satellite could be pointing back towards the radiant by chance. Alternatively, there could be a random meteor that is not part of the shower that originates from a different part of the sky.

There's a more reliable way to distinguish between a meteor and a satellite, as long as you're taking

I took this image at Lily Lake in Rocky Mountain National Park during the Geminids meteor shower. I took repeated 30 second exposures for about four hours until it got cloudy. I then combined every meteor I captured during these exposures into one image. Canon 5D II, 14mm, f2.8, 30 seconds, ISO 1600.

repeated exposures to maximize your chances of capturing a meteor. If you capture something that looks like a meteor, you can check the shot before and after that one to see if the same object is also in those shots. If it is, it's a satellite or airplane gradually moving across the frame of the image. If the object only appears in that one shot and not in any before or after, it's a meteor. Meteors move so fast and die out so quickly that they'll only appear in a single shot.

Even during active meteor showers, it's unlikely that you'll capture more than two meteors in a single frame. While a shot with one or two meteors can be impressive, it doesn't quite capture the essence of a meteor shower, when hundreds of meteors can streak across the sky in a single night. Therefore, many night photographers like to combine every meteor they capture over the course of the night onto a single image.

Accomplishing this is rather straightforward for those experienced with Photoshop. Simply stack every image you took that has a meteor in it onto one file in Photoshop. Then, on all but the very bottom layer, mask out everything except for the individual meteors.

If you do combine all of the meteors into a single image, you'll find that not all meteors point back to the exact same spot in the sky. This is because the radiant will be moving across the sky during the course of the night. Some photographers like to re-orient the meteors so that they are all pointing back to the same spot. This can be easier to do if you include the radiant in the images you shoot. First, locate the approximate location of the radiant in one of the images. You'll then need to rotate all of the other images so that the meteors point back to that radiant. If the North Star is in your image, you can rotate every image around the North Star until the stars in each image line up. If the North Star isn't in your image, you'll have to approximate how much each meteor should be rotated. This isn't an exact science, so you're entitled to some artistic license.

In the image on the previous page, I chose not to rotate the meteors, and therefore they don't all point directly back to one point in the sky.

SATELLITES

As mentioned in the previous section, you can capture streaks of light from a satellite in an image. It might be a stretch to call this a natural light source, but since it's just reflected light from the sun, I'll include it in this chapter.

Some photographers don't like the streaks from satellites and clone them out since they are produced by man-made objects. Other photographers like to include them in the image, and some even plan ahead to try and capture satellites in their images.

You can predict when a satellite will be overhead using a website like http://www.heavens-above.com. This site tells you when you can expect iridium flares and can also tell you where some of the major satellites will be located, including the International Space Station.

COMETS

Comets can produce one of the most dramatic displays in the night sky. Unfortunately, comets that are visible to the naked eye and easy to capture with a DSLR camera are quite rare. However, comets are notoriously unpredictable and some that have yet to be discovered could produce a brilliant display. So if an impressive comet does become visible in the night sky, make sure and photograph it as often as you can because it could be many years or decades before you are presented with another opportunity.

You can use an equatorial mount to capture more detailed images of a comet. This is especially useful if the comet is faint. Using an equatorial mount will be discussed in Chapter IX.

LIGHTNING

Lightning is a spectacular natural phenomenon, but capturing it with a camera can be quite dangerous. I usually try to photograph lightning when the storm is a good distance away and there are no storm clouds directly overhead. Occasionally, though, I will get caught in the middle of a lightning storm that I have to wait out anyway. In this case, I'll often set up my tripod in the back of my vehicle, which has seats that can fold down. I'll then shoot the lightning out of a back window. Cars act as a Faraday cage, which funnels lightning around the outside of the vehicle. You are therefore much safer inside a vehicle than outside (though never 100% safe). If you're unable to set up your camera inside your car and it's not raining, you can set it up directly outside the car window and program it to do repeated exposures while you stay in the car.

Lightning is so bright that it can be easy to overexpose the image. You'll therefore need to use a lower ISO and possibly a smaller aperture than you normally use at night. The exact settings you need will depend on just how intense the lightning storm is and how close you are to it. I recommend starting with ISO 100 and an aperture of f4.0. As long as there are no stars visible above the storm clouds, you don't need to use the rule of 500 to determine exposure times. I recommend exposures of 1-3 minutes for lightning shots taken at night. This will increase your chances of capturing multiple bolts in a single image.

Once you capture a bolt of lightning in your shot, be sure to check your histogram. If you are blowing out any of the highlights, you'll need to use a smaller aperture or lower ISO. If you are significantly underexposing the image, you should switch to a wider aperture or higher ISO. It is better, however, to underexpose the image than to overexpose it.

If you want, you can combine lightning bolts captured in different exposures into a single photograph. The process for doing this is similar to adding multiple meteors into a single image.

To capture this photo of a lightning storm near Alamosa, Colorado, I took repeated two-minute exposures. In most of the exposures, I captured no lightning at all. However, by taking numerous shots, I was able to capture several images with lightning, including this one with two dramatic bolts. Canon 5D, 50mm, f3.5, 142 seconds, ISO 100.

NORTHERN LIGHTS

Of all the sources of light discussed in this chapter, the northern lights (also known as the aurora borealis) may be the most spectacular. This phenomenon is caused by charged particles from the sun interacting with gaseous particles in our atmosphere. These lights also appear in the southern hemisphere, where they are known as the southern lights, or the aurora australis.

The northern lights are more active when sunspot activity is high. For reasons that aren't entirely known, sunspot activity tends to run in cycles lasting approximately 11 years. The last peak of this solar cycle occurred in 2014, and the next solar max should occur around 2025. However, you don't need to wait until peak activity to photograph the northern lights. If you travel up near the Arctic Circle, there's a good chance you will be able to see them any year.

You can view a forecast for the northern lights online at http://auroraforecast.gi.alaska.edu/. This website gives you a general idea of where the northern lights will be visible on any given night. For example, if you are in the northern continental United States, you might be able to see the northern lights if the forecast is 5 or higher. However, to get the best chance of viewing the northern lights, you'll need to travel even farther north. To find the best locations, try to find a day when the forecast on the above website is a 1 or a 2. Anywhere within the bright green circle is a prime viewing spot for the northern lights. Some places that are somewhat easier to access in prime viewing areas are Wiseman, Alaska; Yellowknife, Canada; Iceland and northern Norway.

You can find another northern lights forecast on the Space Weather website at http://swpc.noaa.gov/products/30-minute-aurora-forecast/. This site has more detailed information on auroral activity, but it is harder to learn how to use. There are also free iTunes apps called Aurora Forecast and 3D Sun that alert you when there is a major solar flare that is likely to produce a good northern lights show. For Android users, there's a free app called Aurora Buddy and an inexpensive app called Aurora Alert.

Most of the predictions you'll find for the northern lights are only given a few days in advance. There is, however, a way to predict the aurora nearly a month in advance. If the northern lights are really active one night, there is a chance that they will be active again in 27-28 days. This is because many sunspots rotate around the sun once every 27-28 days. If the sunspot that caused the strong auroral activity is still active the next time it rotates around and faces Earth, there is a good chance the aurora will be stronger than normal. This prediction is, however, far from perfect, as sun spots can fade.

The northern lights are reflected in a lake near Yellowknife, Canada. Nikon D800e, 14mm, f2.8, 13 seconds, ISO 3200.

While it is ideal to photograph the northern lights when they are most active, this isn't as important if you are in a prime viewing area. It's possible you'll see a spectacular show even if the forecast is low. I learned this the hard way on my first night in Wiseman, Alaska. The forecast was just 1, so I decided to get to sleep after a long drive. The next day, the lodge owner told me the auroral display that night was one of the best she'd ever seen. I ignored the

I captured this image at Jokulsarlon lagoon in southern Iceland in September of 2013. On this date, the sun was near the peak of it's 11-year cycle in sunspot activity, so my chances of seeing the northern lights were good. Nikon D800e, 19mm, f2.8, 20 seconds, ISO 3200.

---

forecast the rest of the trip and went out every night as long as I could. I was rewarded with a view of the northern lights every single night.

You may not get as lucky as I did and might have to wait through several long, cold nights for the aurora borealis to show up. But once it does, you'll see a dazzling light show that makes the wait worthwhile. When the light show does erupt, you'll want to work fast getting many different shots and compositions.

To photograph the northern lights, you can rely largely on the techniques and camera settings that I described in Chapter IV. However, if the northern light are moving rapidly in the sky, you'll generally want to limit your exposures to 15 seconds or less. Otherwise, the lights can start to blur too much with longer exposures. Also, when the northern lights are really bright, it is possible to overexpose the shot. I recommend underexposing the images a little, so that you won't risk overexposing the image if the lights suddenly brighten. You'll want to frequently check your histogram to make sure you're not coming close to clipping the highlights. If you are, you'll want to lower the ISO or exposure length.

The northern lights can fill up most of the sky, and I've found that even ultra-wide angle lenses may only capture a portion of the display. I therefore find it useful to do stitched images to capture more of the scene. If the aurora is bright and moving fast, I recommend using a 14mm lens to create a single-row stitched panorama. You'll have to take all of the images pretty quickly. Otherwise, the aurora can move so much that the images won't stitch together seamlessly.

If the aurora is relatively dim, it doesn't tend to move as fast. In this situation, I've found it possible to do multi-row stitched panoramas with up to 20 images. These large stitched images can help minimize noise, which is more noticeable when the aurora is fainter. I usually use a 24mm lens to capture such images.

The best time of the year to photograph the northern lights is near the spring and autumn equinoxes in March and September. The northern lights tend to be somewhat more active during these months than other months. Never plan a trip to photograph the northern lights between late-April and early-August. During this time, it won't got dark for very long, if at all, at the far northern latitudes. If you plan a trip in December or January, it will be dark much of the day, if not all of the day. However, it can be bitterly cold during this time, so spring and autumn is still preferable for all but the most adventurous photographers.

You can shoot the northern lights under almost any moon phase. The aurora will be brighter under no moon, but any foreground in your shot will likely be rendered as a dark silhouette. Under a full moon, the foreground will be well-illuminated and the aurora will be fainter, but this may not matter. The northern lights are often so bright that they will be easily visible under a full moon. My favorite time to shoot the northern lights is under a moon that is 20%-50% illuminated. It will be dark enough to see the stars and aurora a little better than under a full moon, and you'll still be able to render a lot of detail in the foreground. In order to be able to shoot under a variety of conditions, I recommend planning a trip so that you arrive near a new moon and leave near a full moon.

One mistake I've seen photographers make is to go on an expensive trip to see the northern lights without having done any night photography beforehand. They then come away with subpar images that are out of focus or improperly exposed. Unless you live in an area where you can see the northern lights, I recommend becoming proficient in night photography before paying for an expensive trip to see the aurora. Photographing the northern lights is more difficult than photographing most other night scenes. The lights can move fast and may not appear for very long, so you need to be able to make the most of your time when the lights are out. If you practice with easier subjects beforehand, you should be able to come away some great images.

AIRGLOW

Even if you shoot outside of twilight hours when there is no moon out, you may not get perfectly dark skies. Molecules and atoms in the upper atmosphere can emit faint light known as airglow. Airglow is more prominent when the sun is near solar max and there are a lot of sunspots. You can't see airglow with the naked eye, so you will only know that it exists when it shows up in your photographs. It can appear in many different colors but is usually green or red.

Airglow can sometimes appear similar to light pollution. If you see red or yellow colors in the sky and there is a city or town in that direction, it is probably light pollution. If there are no towns in that direction or you see any green colors, it is probably airglow.

ZODIACAL LIGHT

Zodiacal light is caused by sunlight that is reflected off of space dust known as the zodiacal cloud. It appears as a triangular white glow pointing up from the horizon near where the sun has set or where it is about to rise. It is easiest to see around the spring and fall equinoxes, either in late March or late September. Zodiacal light is rather faint, so it is best photographed under no moon and far away from any light pollution.

NOCTILUCENT CLOUDS

Noctilucent clouds are the highest clouds in the atmosphere. They are only visible during twilight, when Earth's shadow covers lower parts of the sky. They are most often seen in the summer at locations between 50 and 70 degrees north and south of the equator.

Lava from Kilauea volcano on the Big Island of Hawaii flows into the Pacific Ocean. Canon 5D, 300mm, f5.6, 0.6 seconds, ISO 640.

Noctilucent clouds are difficult to observe, since they are quite rare. However, they can produce some great photos if you are lucky enough to see them. They generally appear as thin, wispy clouds and can produce intricate patterns in the sky.

LAVA

Lava is one of nature's most brilliant and dramatic phenomena. It is difficult to find, as it requires an active volcano. The Big Island of Hawaii may be the best place to photograph lava, as Kilauea is one of the world's most active volcanos. Its current eruption began in 1983, and it has been active ever since. Even here, though, lava flows can be very unpredictable, and sometimes they will occur in very remote and dangerous places. In this case, it may be easier to photograph from a helicopter or boat around sunset or sunrise or during twilight.

Other places with a lot of volcanic activity include Iceland, Italy, Central America, Indonesia, Papua New Guinea, and Vanuatu. Many of these places are located along the Ring of Fire, which stretches along the edge of the Pacific Ocean where tectonic plates are colliding with one another. You can find news on current volcanic activity throughout the world at http://www.volcanodiscovery.com

It will often be too dangerous to get close to the lava, so you may be shooting from a long distance away. You'll therefore need a long telephoto lens. I recommend having a lens of at least 200mm.

Lava is very bright, and it can be easy to overexpose your images. Also, there can be a lot of rapidly-moving smoke in the air if the lava is entering the ocean. You can use a short exposure of one second or less if you don't want the smoke to be blurred, or you can do a longer exposure if you prefer a blurred look.

The lava may be bright enough that you can rely on the exposure meter on your camera to determine the proper exposure. Always check the histogram after the exposure to make sure you are not blowing out the highlights.

If it's too dark to use your exposure meter, I recommend starting with an exposure of one second using ISO 100 and the widest aperture on your lens. These are very rough settings, as the lava can vary in brightness depending on how much there is, how far away it is, and whether it is obscured by smoke. You'll need to check the histogram and adjust your ISO and shutter speed until you get a shot where there is data throughout the histogram, but you are not clipping the highlights.

FOREST FIRES

While forest fires can be a very destructive force of nature, they can also provide some unique photographic opportunities

Fires can be difficult to photograph, as police and fire fighters will quickly cordon off the area around the fire. Therefore, unless you have special access to an area, they are often best photographed when they occur on a mountainside that can be seen from a long distance away.

If you are close to a fire or using a long telephoto lens, the fire can appear very bright, and I recommend using the same approach to photographing it

I took this shot from the same area as the previous image, but this one was taken shortly after sunset rather than at night. Canon 5D, 300mm, f5.6, 1/4 seconds, ISO 320.

as you would with lava.

If the fire is a long distance away and appears rather faint through your viewfinder, you can use exposure settings closer to what you normally would at night. Just make sure you aren't overexposing the fire.

MOONBOWS

A little-known object that can occasionally can be captured in a photograph is a moonbow. A moonbow is just like a rainbow, but it is created from the light from the moon rather than the sun. When a bright moon is out, moonbows probably occur nearly as often as rainbows, but they are so little known because they can barely be seen with the naked eye.

If the moon comes out during a rainstorm at night, you should look in the opposite direction of the moon to see if you can spot a moonbow. It will appear as a very faint arc, and you won't likely be able to see the colors in it, since you'll be using your rods to see. An easier way to find moonbows is if you photograph a misty waterfall with the moon behind you.

Since moonbows are so faint, you can use camera settings similar to those described in Chapter IV. However, if there are no stars visible, you can ignore the rule of 500 and do longer exposures from 1-3 minutes. In this case, you may need to lower the ISO to avoid overexposing the image.

If you are attempting to photograph lightning in addition to a moonbow, like I did in the image on the next page, you will need to lower your ISO a lot more to avoid overexposing the lightning.

I took this shot while a forest fire raged in Utah's La Sal Mountains. Since I was several miles away from the fire and I was using a wide angle lens, I used only a slightly smaller aperture than I normally would when shooting star trails. Canon EOS 650 film camera, 24mm, f4.0, 2 hours, ISO 100.

BIOLUMINESCENCE

Bioluminescence is the production of light by a living organism. It can be produced on land by things like fireflies, glowworms, and fungi. One of the best places to see and photograph bioluminescence on land is the Waitomo Glowworm Caves in New Zealand.

Bioluminescence occurs much more frequently in the ocean, where many deep sea creatures produce light. These animals are very difficult to photograph, as they rarely come near the water's surface. One place where they can be seen from land is in Toyama Bay, Japan. Millions of Firefly Squid surface along the beach during mating season from March to June.

Perhaps the best opportunity to photograph bioluminescence is when it is produced by phytoplankton known as dinoflagellates. Dinoflagellates can thrive in areas with a lot of algae. If the algal bloom is large enough, they can cover the ocean surface with a neon blue color at night.

Mosquito Bay in Puerto Rico is thought to have the world's largest concentration of dinoflagellates and may therefore be the best place to photograph bioluminescence. Halong Bay in Vietnam is another good place to see this phenomenon. It's not as bright as in Mosquito Bay, but Halong Bay is one of the most scenic bays in the world, making it a great place to photograph both day and night. Vaadhoo Island in the Maldives also has large concentrations of dinoflagellates.

Some good places to see bioluminescent waters in the United States are Manasquan Beach in New Jersey and Mission Bay in San Diego. In Europe, Norfolk, UK is a good place to view this phenomenon.

Dinoflagellates shine brightest when they are in motion. So they can be easier to photograph along a breaking wave. You can also wade in the waters yourself to stir them up.

The bioluminescence you'll find along ocean shores isn't overly bright, so you can use the same camera settings as detailed in Chapter IV.

When I captured this image of a moonbow in Castle Valley, Utah, I was attempting to photograph lightning during an intense storm. I didn't actually see the moonbow until it started showing up as a faint arc on my camera's LCD screen. I used a low ISO in order to avoid overexposing any bright lightning. *Canon 5D, 29mm, f4.0, 92 seconds, ISO 200.*

VI. Light Painting

So far, I've only discussed how to capture images at night using natural light sources. If you're unable to get the shot you want using natural light, you can illuminate the foreground using a flashlight or other artificial light. This is known as light painting, since you are effectively "painting" the scene with strokes of light.

Although light painting can help you capture some stunning images at night, I believe that it can be overdone. Oftentimes, when a photographer first goes out to photograph at night, they will illuminate every photograph using a flashlight. This is a natural thing to do, as humans often need a flashlight to see at night and therefore it may help a camera to "see" at night as well. However, modern cameras can pick up a lot more detail than humans can see with the naked eye. You can get very good results without a flashlight. In fact, all but two images in this book outside of this chapter was shot without the use of a flashlight. So I discourage anyone from only doing light painting when first going out to photograph at night. I think it is better to discover what the camera is capable of without a flashlight and then use a flashlight when you feel that you can't get the shot you want without one.

When I want to light up a foreground subject, I will usually attempt to time it so that a crescent moon will be in the right part of the sky to illuminate it. This will generally produce more natural-looking photographs than a flashlight. I discussed this in more detail Chapter II.

There are, however, locations, such as caves or alcoves, where the moon will never light up the foreground. There are also times when you won't want the moon to be out, as you will want the darkest sky possible to capture more dramatic shots of celestial objects, like the Milky Way, meteors, or zodiacal light. In this case, you have two main options if you want to illuminate the foreground - you can light paint the scene or you can blend multiple exposures, which I will discuss in Chapter IX.

The first option is generally easier, as blending multiple exposures requires some expertise in Photoshop. Light paintings can also benefit from extra work in Photoshop to make them appear more natural, but this usually won't require as much time or expertise.

Another benefit of light painting is that you can control exactly where you want the source of light to be and how the light and shadows will appear on the object you are photographing. A disadvantage is that it is difficult to illuminate both near and distant objects evenly in a photograph. The foreground will usually be illuminated, and the distant background (if there is any) will be dark. This can result in unnatural-looking shots.

Light painting can be used in more creative ways that are limited only by the imagination. Using light painting to create such images will not be discussed much in this chapter, as the focus of this book is on capturing photographs at night that look more natural.

LIGHTING EQUIPMENT

Before you try light painting, you'll need to decide what light source you want to use to capture your images. There are countless options to

---

Left: I used a flashlight to illuminate an alcove in Utah containing several Anasazi Indian ruins. I positioned the flashlight to the left of the camera in order to create shadows in the alcove and give a better sense of its size and depth. Nikon D800e, 16mm, f2.8, 30 seconds, ISO 3200.

I made one of my first attempts at light painting at Delicate Arch in Utah. In order to capture a wide variety of images, I also took several shots with no light painting, where the arch appeared as a silhouette. Canon 5D, 24mm, f1.6, 25 seconds, ISO 1600.

choose from. I'll discuss a couple lights that I use, along with several others that can work well for night photography. I've listed a lot of options for avid light painters who want as much versatility as possible. However, most people will only need one of the smaller flashlights to get good results with light painting.

Flashlights

Flashlights are well-suited for light painting, as they are usually light and portable. Flashlights with adjustable focus are useful, as they can put out a narrow beam or a wide, diffuse beam. A wide beam is generally more useful for light painting, but you can switch to a narrower beam if you want to shine a brighter, more concentrated light on distant objects.

The most powerful flashlights don't usually have adjustable focus. To get a wider beam with these, you can purchase a diffuser. If there isn't a diffuser made specifically for your flashlight, just make sure the one you buy is wide enough to fit over the flashlight. If you don't want to purchase a diffuser, you can instead cut out part of a one-gallon plastic water bottle and tape this in front of the flashlight. This may not be quite as effective as a diffuser, but it is less expensive and more customizable.

Some flashlights I recommend are:

LED Lenser P7 LED Flashlight

I use this flashlight for most of my light paintings. It costs around $40, weighs eight ounces, and has adjustable focus. There's also a newer version of this flashlight called P7.2 that costs about $60.

The original version has two brightness settings, which can produce as much as 175 lumens. I like using the dimmest setting to illuminate nearby objects up to 100 feet away without the risk of overexposing the image. The brightest setting can be used for objects up to about 400 feet away.

The Lenser flashlight uses LED bulbs. Some advantages to LED bulbs are that they last longer and use less energy than any other bulb, thus increasing battery life. A disadvantage is that many LED bulbs, including the ones in this flashlight, cause the images to have an unnatural-looking blue tint. However, if you're proficient with Photoshop, you can quickly select the part of the image that is lit by the flashlight and adjust the colors to your taste. Alternatively, you could process the image with two different white balances - one for the light painted part of the image and one for the rest of the image - and then blend them in Photoshop.

If you want to avoid extra work in post-processing, you can put a warm filter in front of the flashlight to change the color of the light. This will make the light a little less bright and may reduce the range to around 300 feet. I'll discuss filters you can buy later in this chapter.

I've listed the name of the Lenser flashlight that I use, but really any Coast or Lenser brand flashlight with adjustable focus and more than one brightness setting will work.

Vizeri VZ230

This flashlight is similar to the Lenser, but it does have some features that the Lenser does not have. The manufacturer states that this is the only waterproof flashlight with adjustable focus. Also, this flashlight comes with a diffuser, which can be useful if you want to illuminate close objects with a very diffuse light. It is even smaller than the Lenser, yet it is still very powerful and can produce 230 lumens. The Vizeri costs around $50. Like the Lenser, this flashlight uses LED bulbs that have a cool, blue light.

EagleTac G25C2 MKII Neutral White

This is a very bright, compact flashlight that can put out 1180 lumens. This will likely be too bright for most of your light painting needs. However, it can be useful for light painting distant objects up to about 1,000 feet away. It is dimmable to just eight lumens, so you can use it for very close objects as well. This flashlight uses a neutral white LED bulb, meaning that it puts out a warmer light than most LEDs. You therefore won't need to adjust the colors as much, if any, in post-processing. It doesn't have adjustable focus, but it puts out a relatively broad, even light. If you need a wider beam, you can purchase the EagleTac G25C2 Flip-Over Filter Assembly with Diffuser and Color Lens. This flashlight is somewhat expensive and currently sells for a little over $100.

EagleTac D25C Clicky Neutral White

This is another flashlight made by EagleTac that puts out a warmer light from an LED bulb. It retails for $75 and is a very small flashlight, weighing just one ounce without a battery. Despite its size, it puts out a very impressive 317 lumens and is dimmable down to just one lumen. Like the G25C2, it puts out a fairly broad light but doesn't have adjustable focus. You can buy a diffuser that is made for this flashlight.

Luminar Work 69286 Rechargeable Spotlight

This spotlight uses a halogen bulb that puts out a warm light. The beam is fairly narrow, so you'll likely need to use a diffuser with it. It isn't dimmable, so it could be easy to overexpose nearby objects with this light. I personally prefer lights that are dimmable and that have adjustable focus. I've listed this spotlight because it sells for just over $10 at http://www.harborfreight.com, making it a good option if you're on a budget and want a warm light that produces natural colors.

Nitecore Tiny Monster TM26

If you're looking for a lightweight but extremely bright flashlight, the Nitecore may be for you. It weighs about a pound and has five different brightness settings, ranging from just three lumens up to an amazing 3800 lumens. This could allow you to light paint objects a half-mile away.

This flashlight puts out a relatively wide beam for such a bright light, which can be good for night photography. You may, however, want to use it with a diffuser to get an even wider beam. As with many LED flashlights, it does put out a cool blue color, and you will likely need to adjust the color in post-processing or use a color filter.

This flashlight will set you back about $300 and you'll be paying another $100 for the batteries.

Given the high price, it may only be suitable for the most avid light painters. Although the super bright light may be fun to use, it is not easy to get natural-looking shots with it. It can be difficult to evenly illuminate the entire scene, and you can easily overexpose any close foreground objects. For really distant objects, I think it's better to have the moon illuminate the scene or blend multiple exposures, as described in Chapter IX.

Instead of using this flashlight to illuminate distant objects, you can point it straight up and create a bright beam of light stretching into the heavens. While this certainly won't create natural-looking shots, it can make for a dramatic image.

LED Panels

An LED panel can put out a very wide, diffuse

This image shows the Milky Way behind Double Arch in Arches National Park. I light painted the underside of the arch with a Lenser flashlight in order to bring out some of the texture and color in the arch. In post-processing, I used a Burn/Dodge layer to tone down any bright spots and make the lighting appear even throughout the arch. Nikon D800e, 14mm, f2.8, 30 seconds, ISO 6400.

VI. Light Painting

I took this shot of Uranium Arch near Moab, Utah on an autumn night. I was standing inside an alcove, and there was no way the moon could have illuminated the interior of this arch. I therefore decided to illuminate it with a flashlight on a moonless night. Since the skies were very dark with no moon, I was able to capture more detail in the Milky Way. Nikon D800e, 14mm, f2.8, 25 seconds, ISO 3200.

---

beam, which can fill your entire camera frame. Although it is primarily used by videographers and portrait photographers, it can also be useful for night photography. Since it puts out such a broad light, you can use it if you want to create a stitched image or a focus-stacked image and need to make sure each frame is illuminated the same. However, for small stitched images and most focus stacked images, I have found that you can do this with any broad, diffuse flashlight, as long as you're careful to evenly illuminate every part of the scene in each shot. For larger stitched images, it can be difficult to get even lighting in every frame, and the LED panel can be more useful.

A disadvantage of an LED panel is that it is so diffuse that it's to difficult control how much light hits different parts of the scene. As I'll dis-

cuss later in this chapter, you want to spend more time light painting more distant parts of the foreground. Since you can't do this as easily with an LED panel, the nearest objects may appear significantly brighter than more distant objects. This can be fixed to some extent in Photoshop, but to get the best shot with the least amount of noise, it's better to get an image close to how you want it to look in camera. As a result, I don't recommend this as your primary light and only recommend it for more avid light painters who want different lighting options.

A good LED panel is:

Neewer 160 LED Panel

This panel can currently be purchased on Amazon

for under $30, making it a great value. It weights under one pound, is dimmable, and comes with filters that can make the light warmer or more diffuse.

Strobes

Unlike an LED panel, which puts out a continuous beam of light, a strobe puts out one quick, bright burst of light. Like the LED, it puts out a broad, diffuse light that may be useful for stitched images or focus stacking. You do, however, have even less control over how much light hits different parts of the scene. The foreground will likely appear much brighter than the background, so it's better to use if objects in your shot are all about the same distance from the camera.

Perhaps the best use for a strobe light is if you want to include people in the shot and there is no moon out. Rather than having them stand perfectly still for the entire exposure, they will only need to stay still during the quick burst of light from the strobe. In order to even out the light in the scene, you may also want to use a flashlight to light paint more distant objects. Just make sure not to shine the flashlight near the spot the person is standing or the person could look like a ghost in the photograph.

A strobe I recommend is:

Britek PS-200B Battery Powered Strobe Light

This strobe isn't extremely bright, but it is brighter than most camera flashes and can illuminate objects up to about 100 feet away at night. It costs under $70 and comes with a strobe reflector, which can fill in some of the harsh shadows that are created by strobes. You may want to purchase a softbox, which covers the strobe and creates a more diffuse light.

If you want a brighter, battery-powered strobe, you'll probably be paying several hundred dollars. I don't think it's worthwhile to pay that much for a strobe for light painting, as you'll likely only have use for it in limited situations.

Another option if you already own a flash is to just use the flash off-camera.

Headlamps

I primarily use a headlamp for hiking at night. However, headlamps have improved so much that they can also be used for light painting. I use a headlamp as a backup for light painting in case my main flashlight stops working or I forget to bring it. I recommend buying a headlamp that can put out both a diffuse beam, as well as a narrow one.

Since this petroglyph panel was very close to me, I used a dim setting on my Coast headlamp to illuminate it. Nikon D800e, 17mm, f2.8, 20 seconds, ISO 3200.

I took this photo on the slopes of Mount Bross in Colorado while unsuccessfully trying to capture a bright meteor from the Perseids shower. Since there was no moon out on this night, I stood about 15 feet to the right of the camera and used a flashlight to illuminate the bristlecone pines. Canon 5D II, 14mm, f2.8, 30 seconds, ISO 3200.

A headlamp I recommend is:

Coast HL7 Focusing LED Headlamp

This headlamp is useful because it has adjustable focus. You can use a more concentrated beam when hiking and a broader beam for light painting. It puts out an impressive 196 lumens and is dimmable down to just three lumens.

The dimming function can be very useful if you want to light paint very close subjects. If you used a standard flashlight or spotlight that can't be dimmed as much, it could be too bright, causing you to overexpose the image. If you tried to fix this by only shining the flashlight on the subject for a couple of seconds, you might not have time to evenly illuminate the whole scene. The headlamp may be a better option in this situation if you dim it down to a low setting. You can spend a long time light painting the subject, ensuring more even light across the image.

Campfire

If you will be camping while taking photos, your campfire can act as a good source of light for light painting. It will cast a warm, diffuse light that is fairly natural looking. You'll want to strategically build your campfire so that it will evenly illuminate the front of the objects you plan to photograph. Like the LED panel and strobe, you won't have much control over how the light hits the scene. It works best if the foreground objects you are illuminating are all about an even distance from the campfire.

Color Filters

Color filters can be used to change the color of your light. If you have an LED flashlight, you can use a yellow or orange filter to warm up the light. This can help produce more natural-looking colors straight out of the camera. If you find a color that works best with your flashlight, you can tape the filter onto the flashlight.

Rosco makes swatchbooks with a very large number of color gel filters. They are intended to provide sample colors for people looking to buy much larger sheets. However, the samples themselves can be very useful for light painting. These swatchbooks can be purchased for a very low price. A couple I recommend are:

Roscolux Swatchbook

This sample pack of color gel filters contains more colors than you could ever use and is currently available from BHPhotoVideo.com for just $2.50! These filters are 1.75" x 2.75", so they may not be big enough to cover larger flashlights.

Rosco Cinegel Swatchbook (Large) 3x5"

If the standard swatchbook is not large enough to cover your flashlight, these filters may do the trick. They currently sell for $25 on BHPhotoVideo.com.

EXPOSURE

When light painting, you can generally use camera settings similar to those detailed in Chapter IV. Unless you are using a very bright flashlight or are very close to the subject, it can be difficult to overexpose the image. I recommend starting with an ISO of 3200 and your widest aperture. You will want to keep an eye on the histogram to make sure you are not overexposing the image. If you are, you can use a dimmer setting on your flashlight or simply spend less time painting the area that was overexposed. If neither of these options work, you could lower the ISO.

Another option when light painting is to blend two exposures - one of the light painted part of the scene and one of the night sky. You can do a longer exposure of 1-3 minutes with a lower ISO for the light painting. This will allow you to spend more time painting the scene. This can be especially useful for difficult light paintings, where you need to illuminate close and distant objects. You can also get higher quality images of the land with the longer exposures. Blending multiple exposures will be discussed in Chapter IX.

Before taking your first shot, you may want to close the eyepiece. If light from your flashlight hits the back of the camera, a small amount of light could leak into the eyepiece and affect the image. Some photographers like to close the eyepiece for every photo they take at night. While this may be a worthwhile precaution, I've never had problems with a light leak with exposures under one minute where no flashlight was used. If your camera doesn't allow you to close the eyepiece, you can instead put a cloth or hat over it.

PAINTING TECHNIQUES

There are different techniques you can use to illuminate the scene. Unless you want a more artistic effect, the main goal will be to get diffuse, even light over the subject.

Direct Light

The majority of your light paintings will likely be done with direct light. This simply means that

VI. Light Painting

This image shows the northern lights above Jokulsarlon lagoon in southern Iceland. Even though there was no moon out on this night, the white icebergs were so bright that they were able to reflect light from the northern lights and any other available light. I decided to use a flashlight to add just a bit more light to the nearest icebergs. This reduced the noise in the icebergs and helped them stand out more from those in the distance. Nikon D800e, 18mm, f2.8, 20 seconds, ISO 3200.

---

you will shine the flashlight directly onto the object you are photographing.

I find that using small, rapid circular or side-to-side motions with your flashlight as you light paint is a good way to get even light throughout the photograph. You'll want to move your flashlight over every part of the scene you want illuminated while making these smaller motions. You don't want to hold your flashlight perfectly still for any period of time, as this will produce uneven lighting and can cause parts of the scene to be overexposed.

It's important to spend more time light painting distant objects that you want illuminated than nearby objects. Every time you double the distance to an object, it will receive only 1/4 the amount of light from the flashlight. So you'll need to light paint the object four times longer than an object that is 1/2 the distance away in order to evenly illuminate both objects. If you have a flashlight with adjustable focus, you can use a narrower beam to focus more light on distant objects and a wider beam for nearby objects.

Although this may sound complicated, you don't have to be too exacting. The most important thing is to make sure that everything you want illuminated has been well lit by the flashlight. If some of the areas appear too bright, this is not a problem, as long as you're not blowing out the highlights. You can easily tone down bright spots using a Burn/Dodge layer in Photoshop, which I will describe in Chapter X. If, on the other hand, some parts of the scene are not properly illuminated and are too dark, this is much more difficult to fix. If you try to brighten these areas up later, it will bring out a lot of noise in the image.

If you're unable to get everything lit in one shot, you can try taking several exposures and lighting different parts of the scene in each image. You can then stack all of the exposures on a single file in Photoshop and blend the parts of each image that are properly lit. Blending multiple exposures is discussed in detail in Chapter IX.

It is important to frequently check the photos you are taking on your LCD screen. Make sure you have illuminated every object you intended to light paint during the exposure.

Bounce Light

One way to get more diffuse light in an image is to bounce the light off a rock or other object that is not in the photograph, rather than shining it directly onto the object you are photographing. This is usually best done when you have near foreground objects you want to illuminate. Bounce light can significantly reduce the intensity of the beam, so it can be difficult to use bounce light with distant objects unless you have a very powerful flashlight.

Using bounce light can change the color of the light from your flashlight, depending on the color of the object you're bouncing the light off of. For example, if you are bouncing the light off of an orange rock, it will make the light warmer.

You can experiment bouncing light off many different objects, including rocks, trees, grass, buildings, roads, or even your hand. The diffuseness and color of the beam will vary depending on what you bounce it off.

Fill Light

You will normally want to light paint when there is no moon out, as the moon is bright enough that you won't usually need a flashlight. However, sometimes the moon can cast overly dark shadows on the scene. In this situation, it can be helpful to use a flashlight to provide fill light. You won't need to shine the flashlight over the entire scene. Instead, just focus on getting some light in the shadow areas.

You can also use fill light if there is no moon out and the foreground is very bright or reflective. In this case, you may be able to capture detail in the foreground without a flashlight. However, you might want to use fill light to add a little more light to selective parts of the photo, as I did in the image on the previous page.

Try Different Angles

I recommend shining the flashlight from different angles and positions. You might try a shot with the flashlight positioned near the camera but also try shots with the flashlight to the left and right of the camera. This will produce some shadows and can give the appearance of more depth in the image. It can also bring out more texture in foreground objects.

If you have both near and distant objects you want to illuminate, you can try positioning the flashlight far back from the camera. This will reduce the relative distance between the near and far objects and make it easier to illuminate the entire scene evenly.

Another thing you can experiment with is to position the flashlight in front of the camera. You don't necessarily want light from the flashlight to hit the camera directly. Instead, you can position the flashlight behind a rock or a tree where it is not directly visible from the camera and then illuminate part of the scene with it. This usually won't produce very natural-looking images, but it can produce interesting artistic effects.

If you will be shining the flashlight far from the camera, you can use a self-timer set to 10 seconds or more to give yourself time to get in position before the exposure starts. If this doesn't give you enough time, you can program a longer delay if you have an intervalometer. Or you can simply set your camera to take repeated exposures. You can then move around as much as you want and try painting from different angles and positions, knowing that all along your camera will be taking shots. Another option is to invest in a wireless remote trigger that will allow you to begin an exposure from a good distance away.

Including People

Another way to capture dramatic images with a flashlight is to take an image with you or a friend standing in the photo with a flashlight or headlamp. You can shoot images like this when the moon is out, so that it illuminates the rest of the scene. Another option is to use two flashlights - one concentrated light that the person in the image will be holding and a more diffuse light used by the photographer to illuminate the scene. Or you can have the person standing in the shot use a diffuse flashlight to illuminate part of the scene under no moon and let the rest of the scene remain dark.

I couldn't quite get the shot I wanted of Musselman Arch in Canyonlands National Park. So I decided to stand on the arch and shine a headlamp in order to give some scale to the image and add more drama to the scene. The landscape was illuminated by the moon, and the constellation Orion is rising above me. Nikon D800e, 18mm, f2.8, 20 seconds, ISO 3200.

VII. Star Trails

If you take a very long exposure of the night sky using a camera that is sitting stationary on a tripod, you will capture what are known as star trails. During the course of the exposure, the earth will rotate on its axis and the stars will appear to move across the sky. The camera captures the light from the stars as they move, and the stars appear as curved lines in your image, rather than points of light.

Some people do not like star trails because the image doesn't look like anything you would ever see with the naked eye. I find star trails interesting because the camera provides a representation not just of the spatial dimensions but also of the dimension of time.

Since star trails take such a long time to photograph, I'll oftentimes shoot with more than one camera. With one or even two cameras, I will shoot star trails. While waiting on these shots, I'll take a lot of short exposures with a digital camera.

If you choose to set up multiple cameras, I recommend trying to find unique compositions for each shot. You can even set up your cameras miles apart from one another and leave one while it is taking a long exposure. Of course, you should make sure there is no rain or snow in the forecast and that your camera is in a remote spot where it's not likely to be stolen.

Capturing an image of star trails is a seemingly straightforward process, as you just need to take a really long exposure at night. However, with digital cameras this becomes problematic because, for reasons I will explain later in this chapter, the star trails appear fainter and fainter the longer you expose the shot. Really long exposures also produce large amounts of dark noise. This noise is minimal during shorter exposures, but it increases at a rate proportional to the exposure time. Long Exposure Noise Reduction can help reduce the noise, but it will still be noticeable.

Fortunately, there are a couple of ways around these problems. One is to take a lot of shorter exposures with a digital camera and combine them. The other, less complicated way, is to use a film camera.

I'll go over how to capture images with both a film and digital camera later but will start with something you should consider before ever taking a shot.

PREVISUALIZING THE IMAGE

When composing a shot, it's good to be able to previsualize how the star trails will appear in the image. I've summarized below how star trails will look when you are facing different directions. This information is for photographing in the northern hemisphere. For shots in the southern hemisphere, simply face in the opposite direction to capture star trails like those described below. For example, you can capture star circles when facing due south in the southern hemisphere rather than due north.

Facing North

If you face north when shooting a long exposure at night, you will capture star circles, as seen in the image to the left. The bright star near the very center is Polaris, or the North Star. Since this star is always located due north in the sky, its position will move very little during the night. All of the other stars will appear to rotate around it.

The farther north you are, the higher in the sky the North Star will be. In fact, the angle that the North Star appears in the sky corresponds exactly to the latitude from which you are taking the shot.

To locate the North Star, you first need to find the Big Dipper. The Big Dipper is one of the most prominent star patterns in the sky. As its name suggests, it looks like a giant dipper or ladle, and it will always be in the northern part of the sky. You need to locate the two

---

Left: By positioning my camera so that it was pointing due north, I was able to capture the apparent motion of the stars around Polaris. Minolta 9xi film camera, 28mm, f4.0, 2 1/2 hours, ISO 100.

stars that form the rightmost edge of the Big Dipper (or if the Big Dipper appears upside down in the sky, these stars will be on the leftmost side). These stars point almost directly to the North Star. Simply draw an imaginary line from the two stars and extend it up from the Big Dipper about five times the distance between these two stars to find the North Star.

If the Big Dipper is below the horizon or if it is obscured by clouds, you can also find the North Star using the constellation Cassiopeia. Cassiopeia looks like a big W in the sky, and it is always on the opposite side of the North Star from the Big Dipper. Take the center star in the W and the one just to the left of it (the one just to the right of it if the W is upside down), and draw a line up from the middle star at a 90-degree angle to these two stars. Extend this line about 1 1/2 times the width of the W, and this will lead you to the North Star. The diagram below will make it much easier to visualize this.

You can, of course, use a compass or GPS unit to help you to face due north. This is especially useful if you want to set up a shot before it gets dark. Unless your GPS unit has a compass built into it, it won't be able to determine due north when you are standing still. You will need to walk in the direction you think north is, and it will be able to determine your direction while you are in motion. If you use a compass, you'll need to factor in how many degrees magnetic north is off from true north at the spot you are photographing.

If you want to capture star circles, you should use a wide angle lens in order to capture stars that are well above and below Polaris. I recommend a lens that is at least 30mm wide for a vertical photograph and at least 20mm wide for a horizontal photograph.

I carefully planned this composition to ensure that I was facing due north. I used a wide angle lens so that I could include the entire arch and position Polaris in the center of the shot. Canon EOS 650 film camera, 17mm, f4.0, 2 hours, ISO 100.

When facing north, the stars will appear to move at a slower rate. You'll therefore need a longer exposure to capture sizeable star trails. For most shots, I recommend an exposure of at least two hours.

You can easily find the North Star using either the Big Dipper or Cassiopeia.

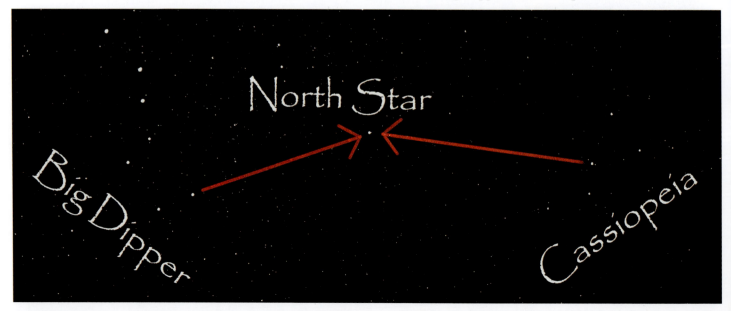

Facing South

If you face south when shooting star trails, the stars will move in shallow arcs across the sky. The farther north you are, the shallower the arcs will appear.

I positioned my camera so that it would be facing due south when photographing this rock formation near Moab, Utah. Canon EOS 650 film camera, f2.8, 2 hours, ISO 100.

Facing East

If you face east, the stars will move up and to your right during the exposure. The star trails will appear as curved, slanted lines. As you travel farther north, the angle of the trails to the horizon will decrease.

When I captured this image of rocks formations in the Garden of Eden in Arches National Park, my camera was pointed east. Minolta 9xi film camera, 24mm, f2.8, 2 hours, ISO 100.

Facing West

If you face west, the stars will move down and to your right during the exposure. Just like when you are facing east, the angle of the star trails to the horizon will decrease as you travel farther north.

I took this shot of Double Arch in Arches National Park while facing west. Minolta 9xi film camera, 16mm fisheye, f2.8, 40 minutes, ISO 100.

Facing Southwest or Southeast

I was facing southwest when shooting this image of Landscape Arch in Arches National Park. From this direction, I was able to capture stars positioned both north and south of the equator. Minolta 9xi film camera, 28mm, f2.8, 2 hours, ISO 100.

If you face toward the southeast or southwest in the

northern hemisphere, you will capture the edges of two circles that are facing away from each other. A star trail located between these two circles falls along the celestial equator. This represents the division between stars positioned south of the equator and stars positioned north of the equator.

As you travel farther north, the celestial equator will become tilted more and more to the south. The point where the celestial equator touches the horizon, however, will always be due east or due west. So if you want the celestial equator to pass through the bottom corner of your image, you will need to position your camera so that the northernmost object in your frame is due east or due west of you.

At the Equator

If you take a shot from a location at or near the equator, the stars will appear as semicircles if you face north or south. If you face east or west, they will appear as nearly-straight, vertical lines. The North Star will be visible just above the horizon if you are slightly north of the equator, and it will not be visible if you are south of the equator.

This image depicts star trails over Arenal Volcano in Costa Rica. Since I was near the equator and facing east when I shot this image, the star trails appear as vertical lines. Canon 5D, 50mm, f2.2, 515 seconds, ISO 100.

At the Poles

It's very unlikely that you'll ever shoot star trails from one of the poles. But if you did, all of the trails from any direction would appear horizontal and parallel to the horizon. At the North Pole, if you look straight up, you will see the North Star, and all of the other stars will be circling around it.

USING A FILM CAMERA

Once you've decided on a location to shoot and have previsualized how the star trails will appear, you'll need to decide how to capture the image. One of the easiest ways to do this is with a film camera.

Choosing a Camera

If you have an old film camera lying around that is gathering dust, you may finally have a use for it. If not, you can purchase a film camera for a very reasonable price. Medium and large format film cameras will produce higher quality images. However, unless you already own such a camera, I recommend using an inexpensive 35mm SLR film camera that is compatible with the lenses for your digital camera. You can find a lot of inexpensive 35mm film cameras on eBay. Ideally, you will want a camera that conserves battery life during the long exposure and doesn't keep a light shining on the display panel the entire time. Otherwise, you will likely be replacing the battery every few exposures. You will also need to buy a remote shutter release for the camera in order to take long exposures.

For Canon EOS shooters, I recommend the Canon EOS 620, 630, or 650 film cameras. These cameras use little battery power during long exposures, so you can take numerous star trail images with a single battery. Each of these cameras requires you to buy a special GR20 grip in order to be able to add a remote shutter release to the camera. You can usually buy the camera, the grip, and the remote shutter release on eBay for around $50.

Unfortunately, I couldn't find a Nikon film camera that works as well as the Canon cameras listed above. The F100 and N80/F80 are the only two reasonably-priced film cameras I found that are fully compatible with G lenses (G lenses are those that don't have a manual aperture ring on them). However, both of these cameras appear to use a lot of battery power during long exposures. You can use the MC-30 Remote Shutter Release with the F100 and will need a threaded cable release for the N80/F80.

The older, fully-manual Nikon film cameras usually don't require a battery to operate, so you don't have to worry about replacing them. Unfortunately, these cameras are not compatible with G lenses. However, every Nikon camera made since 1977 is compatible with the Rokinon lenses since these have manual aperture rings. In fact, any Nikon camera made since 1959 will work with these lenses. The exposure meter won't work properly with pre-1977 cameras, but you don't need the exposure meter for star trails. Among these cameras, I recommend the Nikon FM or FM10, since they are reasonably priced. Some of the other old manual cameras have become collectibles and are rather expensive. You'll need a threaded cable release to take long exposures with these cameras.

Film

The film I recommend is Fuji Provia 100F. This is a super-fine grain slide film that produces more subdued colors than other films in the 100F series. This is important because high saturation films like Velvia are prone to extreme color shifts during long exposures.

There will be noticeable color shift in your images regardless of the film you use. Provia tends to produce purple and pink colors in the sky. I usually find the results pleasing, but you can adjust the colors in post-processing if you don't like them.

Focusing

If possible, you should focus while it is still light out. It's much more difficult to focus film cameras when it's dark. If you use autofocus, make sure to switch your camera to manual focus once you have the focus locked in. Alternatively, if your lens has a hard-stop at infinity and you don't have any close foreground objects, you can just turn the focus ring to infinity.

I used Fuji Provia 100F film to capture a long exposure of these bizarre rock formations in Utah's San Rafael Swell. While waiting on this shot, I used a digital camera to capture a short exposure of the same rocks, which can be seen on page 6. Canon EOS 650, 24mm, f2.8, 2 hours, ISO 100.

If neither of these options works for you, it may be easier to first focus the lens while it is on a digital camera, as described in Chapter IV. You can test the focus by taking a shot on your digital camera. You'll want to use the same aperture you'll be using with your film camera, but you'll need to use a much shorter shutter speed and higher ISO for the test shot. When you have the focus locked in, carefully transfer the lens over to the film camera without moving the focus ring.

Shutter Speed

You can expose the shot as long as you want, from a few minutes for very short star trails to many hours for very long star trails. Rather than time my photos, I usually just pick out a star in the sky and note its position. I then wait for the star to move across the sky and stop the exposure when it has moved about the length I want the star trails to appear.

Alternatively, if you have an intervalometer, you can leave the camera and even go to sleep, as you can be sure the camera will stop exposing once the timer expires. Intervalometers can, however, be difficult to find for film cameras.

If you're using a wide angle lens, I generally recommend exposing for at least two hours to capture long, dramatic star trails. You can do shorter exposures with longer lenses, as the stars won't take as long to move across the frame of your shot. However, the exact exposure length is ultimately your own artistic decision.

Aperture Settings

The aperture you'll use depends primarily on the phase of the moon. The brighter the moon is, the smaller the aperture you'll need. The proper settings for different moon phases are described below.

I captured this image of the Marching Men in Arches National Park on a night when there was no moon out. I was therefore able to use the widest aperture on my lens without fear of overexposing the image. Canon EOS 650 film camera, 28mm, f2.8, 2 hours, ISO 100.

I captured this shot of star trails over West Pawnee Butte in Colorado using a film camera. While I took this shot, I used my digital camera to capture the shot of East Pawnee Butte seen on pages 28-29. Canon EOS 650, 28mm, f2.8, 2 hours, ISO 100.

No Moon

When shooting ISO 100 film on a moonless night, you can use a very wide aperture. There is not much risk of overexposing your photo, as long as you are shooting outside of twilight hours and away from light pollution. I would, however, avoid going wider than f2.8. Wider apertures like f1.4 can produce more vignetting and soft corners, and there's a chance of overexposing the image. If you don't have a fast lens, f4.0 or f5.6 will work for star trails shot with film. The image may be underexposed, but this isn't as big of an issue with film, as you don't have to worry about dark noise.

Crescent Moon

If you want the foreground in your image to be il-luminated, you'll need to shoot with the moon out. I suggest shooting under a moon that is 20%-50% illuminated. A fainter moon may not be bright enough to properly illuminate the foreground, and a brighter moon can cause the shot to be overexposed.

I recommend an aperture setting of f4.0 and an exposure of no more than two or three hours. If you want longer star trails, I recommend an aperture of f5.6 for exposures up to five or six hours and aperture of f6.7 for even longer exposures.

You'll generally want the moon behind you, so it illuminates the front of the foreground object.

Full Moon

If possible, I recommend that you avoid shooting

star trails under a full or gibbous moon with a film camera. The moon is so bright that if you set your aperture to f4.0 or f5.6, you will risk blowing out the highlights after just 15 minutes. One solution to this would be to use a much smaller aperture like f13 and expose for around two hours. The problem with this is that you will get very faint star trails, and the image will look almost like a daytime shot with a blue sky and star trails that are barely visible.

You can usually get better results under a full moon by combining multiple exposures with a digital camera. However, if you do attempt to shoot with a film camera, I recommend using an aperture of f6.7 and an exposure of 15-20 minutes. This should result in an image with clearly visible star trails that aren't overexposed.

Taking the Shot

Once you've decided on your aperture, you should set your film camera to the Bulb setting, which allows you to take very long exposures. Then, simply lock the button on your remote shutter release in place and wait for however long you want to expose the shot. If you have an intervalometer, you can set the length of the exposure beforehand.

Unless you have your own darkroom or film scanner, you'll need to find a photo lab where you can develop and scan the images. Some photo labs no longer develop film, but if you live in a relatively large city you shouldn't have a problem finding a lab that does. Alternatively, you can mail the film to a lab. You can then do post-processing work on the image as described in Chapter X.

One problem with shooting 35mm film is that the number of exposures per roll is usually 36. You'll often only be exposing one image per night, and it may take years to shoot a full roll. So I will often develop partial rolls of film.

USING A DIGITAL CAMERA

Photographing star trails with a digital camera can be more complicated than photographing them with a film camera. It can also be more expensive if you want to shoot with multiple cameras. However, a digital camera can give you the flexibility to later change the appearance of the star trails in post-processing.

When taking these shots, you should start with a fully-charged battery, as it will drain quickly when you are taking long exposures. A battery grip that holds a second battery can be useful.

As I mentioned earlier in this chapter, simply taking a single two-hour exposure with a digital camera can result in lower-quality images. You will usually get better results by taking a lot of short exposures and combining them in Photoshop. I'll go over both of these options below.

Single Exposures

If you take one really long exposure with a digital camera, you'll find that the stars trails appear rather faint compared to a shorter exposure. This is because a single star will only be located at any one point in the sky for a fraction of the length of the exposure. The camera records the light from the star when it is at that spot, but it also records much fainter light from the sky around that star. It records this light during the entire exposure. Over the course of a short exposure, that light is insignificant compared to the star and the star will stand out brightly relative to the rest of the sky. However, over a very long exposure the competing background light becomes more significant. The star stands out less prominently from the rest of the sky and the star trails appear fainter.

One reason you can do longer exposures with film is because of reciprocity failure. Film becomes exponentially less sensitive to light as fewer photons hit it. So the dark areas of the sky between the stars are not easily recorded by film, and the stars will stand out more relative to the rest of the sky.

Another issue with long exposures with a digital camera is that dark noise increases with exposure length. Long Exposure Noise Reduction can help minimize this, and it is especially useful at eliminating hot pixels. However, you will usually still see a red discoloration over parts of the image that can be difficult to eliminate in post-processing.

You'll get less dark noise under a full or gibbous moon. This is because the moon will be so bright that the signal-to-noise ratio will be higher than it is under no moon. However, long exposures taken under a full moon will result in star trails that are even fainter than those taken under no moon.

I recommend limiting single exposures on a digital camera to no more than 15 minutes. If you take longer shots, the noise may increase to unacceptable levels in shots taken under no moon. Under a bright moon, the star trails may become too faint. One exception to this is if you are shooting moon trails, as I'll describe later. In this case, you might prefer fainter trails since the moon is so bright.

I took this shot of Ribbon Arch in Arches National Park with a digital camera as the full moon was rising. Since I was using a telephoto lens, I captured short star trails with just an 80 second exposure. Canon 5D II, 180mm, f4.0, 80 seconds, ISO 1600.

You can always experiment with longer exposures on a digital camera, especially if your goal is to capture fainter star trails. Ultimately, it's up to you to decide how much noise you are comfortable with and how faint you want the star trails to appear.

If you do attempt to capture star trails with a single exposure, be sure to enable Long Exposure Noise Reduction. Your camera will take a dark frame immediately after your shot is exposed, which will help reduce the dark noise in the image. The dark frame will take as long to capture as the original exposure. You will therefore need to make sure you have enough battery power left to complete the dark frame. Also, make sure not to turn your camera off while it is taking the dark frame.

To achieve the best results, the dark frame should be taken in the same conditions as the original shot. Ideally, you should leave your camera at the same spot where you took the shot while it is taking the dark frame. If you don't have enough time or patience for this, you can put it in your car and drive home. The noise reduction may not be quite as effective, but it will be better than nothing. If possible, you should avoid using your heater in order to keep the car temperature similar to the outdoor temperature.

To calculate exposure times and aperture settings for a single exposure, you can start with a test shot using a wide aperture and shorter exposures. You will then need to extrapolate the proper shutter speed and aperture for the longer exposure. For example, let's say you're able to get a good exposure with a shutter speed of 13 seconds at f4.0 and ISO 6400. If you lower the ISO from 6400 to 100, you will be able to shoot 64 times longer. This comes to about 14 minutes. So, you will be able to expose a shot for 14 minutes at f4.0 and ISO 100. If you want to do even longer exposures, you can use smaller apertures. If you close the aperture one stop to f5.6, you will let in half as much light. You can therefore do 28 minute exposures with ISO 100.

You can do the exposure calculations yourself or use an app like PhotoPills for iTunes or Photo Tools for Android. There is no reciprocity failure in digital cameras like there is with film, so you don't need to factor this in when calculating exposure lengths.

Before taking a shot, I recommend closing the eyepiece on your camera to prevent any light leak during the long exposures. If you can't close the eyepiece, you can cover it with a hat or cloth.

Multiple Exposures

Although combining multiple shorter exposures is more complicated than taking a single long exposure, it will almost always produce superior results if your goal is to capture bright, long star trails in your image. You will need to take repeated exposures with your digital camera and later combine them on the computer to create star trails. I'll go over all of the camera settings you need to use to capture these shots and then discuss how to process the images.

Shutter Speed

Perhaps surprisingly, the appearance of star trails will be affected more by the shutter speed you choose than

To capture this image of a balanced rock in Utah, I combined a lot of a short 30-second exposures taken on a digital camera. This allowed me to capture a large number of bright star trails. I took this shot under no moon and used a flashlight to illuminate the foreground. Nikon D800, 24mm, f3.2, 30 secs per exposure, ISO 6400, 48 exposures combined.

---

by your ISO or aperture settings. Shorter individual exposures will yield brighter star trails than longer individual exposures. This may seem counterintuitive because it would be logical to think that combining 90 one-minute exposures would be basically the same as combining 30 three-minute exposures. However, the star trails will appear brighter in the image made from 90 one-minute exposures.

As explained in the section on single exposures, longer exposures will produce fainter star trails than shorter exposures. So the stars will be fainter in a three-minute exposure than a one-minute exposure relative to the rest of the sky. You might think that this would be offset when you combine the 90 one-minute exposures vs. just 30 three-minute exposures. In the final image, each star trail will have been exposed for 90 minutes and the star trails will appear the same length in both images. This would be the case if the software you used to create the star trails simply averaged the brightness levels in each exposure, similar to how a camera records data over a period of time. However, the software doesn't work this way.

When blending two images, stacking software used to create star trails typically only uses the brightest pixels from one image and discards the darker pixels in the other image. If there is a bright star in a certain spot in one image but not the other, it will keep the data from that star and discard data from the other image. This will make the star nearly twice as bright as it would have been if the software had simply averaged the brightness of the pixels in each image. The more images you combine, the brighter the stars will be compared to an image where you simply average the values of all of the pixels. This will make it look like there are more star trails in the image, but this is largely an illusion. It only appears this way because the faint star trails stand out more.

If this sounds overly complicated, don't worry. All you need to know is that shorter individual exposures will produce brighter star trails than longer exposures.

The exact exposure length you choose is ultimately an artistic decision. Thirty-second exposures shot under no moon will produce a large number of bright star trails packed together. Some people like all the streaks of light and think it adds drama to the photo. Others feel that this makes the image look too busy and overcrowded. I personally prefer fewer bright star trails in most of my images. However, I do occasionally like to have a very large number of bright star trails. It can create a dizzying, almost mesmerizing effect, especially if you are facing north. For these shots, you may want to limit the total exposure length to 30 minutes or less. The individual star trails will be shorter, but you will capture so many bright star trails that the image will still appear to be packed with stars. If you do longer exposures, there can be too many bright star trails and some may overlap with each other.

If you want to capture long star trails under no moon with a total exposure length of around two hours, I find that shutter speeds of 2-3 minutes work well. There won't be as many bright star trails, so they won't appear to be packed together as tightly. You can increase the length of the individual exposures to around five minutes if you want even fainter trails. I don't generally recommend doing longer individual exposures, as the dark noise can become more problematic.

If you shoot under a moon, the star trails will appear fainter, so you may want to compensate by using shorter individual exposures. I like using individual exposures of around 1-2 minutes under a quarter moon and 15-30 seconds under a full moon.

You need to minimize the time between each exposure, so as to avoid having a noticeable gap in the star trails. On your intervalometer, you should set the interval between exposures to one second. Make sure Long Exposure Noise Reduction, mirror lockup, and the self-timer are all off on your camera. These functions will increase the time between each exposure.

If you don't have an intervalometer, you can use a standard remote shutter release and take repeated exposures up to 30 seconds each. However, many cameras limit the number of shots you can take in continuous-shooting mode. So make sure your camera will be able to continue shooting as long as you want.

Another option for taking repeated exposures is to use the interval timer that is built into many of Nikon's DSLRs and that you can add to Canon EOS cameras with the Magic Lantern software. When using Nikon's timer for 30 second exposures, you should set the interval to 33 seconds. The reason for doing this was discussed on page 21.

Aperture Settings

The aperture you choose actually won't have too much effect on the appearance of the final image. If you use a really wide aperture, you will get a brighter image, and if you use a smaller aperture, you will get a darker image. However, the relative brightness of the stars to the rest of the sky will stay the same. Therefore, if you adjust the brightness of the images in post-processing so they match each other, they will look very similar.

For short exposures where you want the stars rendered as points of light, it is important to use a very wide aperture to reduce noise. This isn't quite as important when stacking images to create star trails. Since you will be combining so many images, you will effectively be increasing the signal-to-noise ratio and can get good quality images with smaller apertures. I therefore recommend stopping down from the widest aperture to get closer to the sweet spot of your lens. The sweet spot is where your lens performs best if noise is not as big of an issue. It will produce less vignetting and can make the images a little sharper.

For a lens with a maximum aperture of f1.4, I recommend shooting at f2.8 or f3.2. For a lens with a maximum aperture of f2.8, I recommend shooting star trails at f5.6. For a lens with a maximum aperture of f4.0 or smaller, I recommend shooting at f6.3 or f6.7.

The smaller apertures will also give you more depth of field and allow you to include closer foreground objects in the image. If necessary, you can use even smaller apertures to further increase depth of field.

ISO

As with most night shots, you can use the highest native ISO on your camera that doesn't cause you to blow out any of the highlights in the image. If you're shooting under a bright moon, you may need to lower the ISO significantly to avoid overexposing the photo. Also, if the moon will be rising during the course of your exposures, you will want to underexpose the initial image to ensure that it does not become overexposed after the moon rises.

As with the aperture setting, the ISO you choose won't significantly affect the final appearance of the image. Any ISO between 800-6400 will produce about the same results. Higher ISOs will not produce brighter star trails relative to the rest of the sky. ISOs below 800 can start to show more noise, so you should avoid them unless shooting under a bright moon.

Taking the Shots

Before you begin your exposures, you should take a test shot with the camera settings you have decided on. Review the test shot on your LCD screen to make sure everything is in focus and you are not overexposing the image.

If the test shot looks good, I recommend taking a single dark frame with the lens cap and eyepiece cover on. Be sure to use the same settings that you will be using with all of the other shots. The dark frame can help reduce noise in the image in post-processing.

You can now begin taking continuous exposures of the scene. You'll need to take the lens cap back off, but you can keep the eyepiece closed to prevent light leak. If you are using an intervalometer or built-in timer, you can set the exact number of exposures that the camera will take. If you're not sure how many exposures you want to take, you can set this to the maximum value or to --. You can then manually stop the exposures whenever you want.

I recommend beginning the exposures around the end of nautical twilight, or about 50 minutes after sunset.

At this time, it should still be light enough to capture detail in the foreground, even under no moon. If you find that the images you took during this time are too bright and cause the sky to look washed out, you can always eliminate the first several exposures when you are combining the images in post-processing. So it is better to start shooting a little too early than too late.

Another option for getting detail in the foreground is to take one exposure shortly after sunset. You can combine the foreground from this shot with the star trails you capture later in the evening. Combining multiple exposures will be explained in detail in Chapter IX.

Once you start taking the continuous exposures, you can just sit back and wait as long as necessary to capture the length of star trails you desire. It's better to shoot too many shots than too few, as you can always shorten the star trails later. If you're using a wide angle lens, I recommend letting the camera continue shooting for at least a couple of hours (or until the battery dies). If you are using a longer lens, you can do shorter exposures and still capture long star trails.

Post-Processing with Digital

There are many ways to create a composite image with star trails after you capture all of your photos. One way is to simply stack all of the images you took onto a single file in Photoshop and change the blending mode of the layers to Lighten. Unfortunately, because of the way the Lighten blending mode works, this will leave gaps in the star trails, and they will look like dotted lines. You can avoid this problem by using a combination of the Lighten blending mode and the Screen blending mode. This is a somewhat complicated process, but fortunately Floris Van Breugel has created a free Photoshop script that does all of the work for you. This script can be found at http://www.artinnaturephotography.com/page/startrailstacker/

When preparing files in Lightroom to be used with this script, you can select the first image you plan to use in the star trail sequence. First, you'll want to set the white balance at a temperature that looks natural to you. Then you should move the Exposure slider to the left to intentionally underexpose the image. You'll want to keep almost all of the data on the left half of the histogram and leave the right half mostly

I captured this image of Skyline Arch in Arches National Park by combining a lot of shorter exposures on a digital camera. I created a comet-like effect by progressively decreasing the opacity of the layers to make the star trails slowly taper off. I did not, however, add glowing heads to these star trails. Nikon D800e, 14mm, f5.6, 3 minutes per exposure, ISO 1600, 20 exposures combined.

---

empty. This is an important step which isn't mentioned in the instructions provided with this script. If you don't do this, the final image produced by the stacking software may have blown highlights.

If you see chromatic aberration in the stars, you can try to fix this by adjusting the sliders under Color in the Lens Correction panel. All of the other adjustment sliders including Sharpening should set to zero, and the Tone Curve should be set to Linear. These settings will help ensure that you get the smoothest possible star trails. You'll only want to make adjustments to contrast, saturation, vignetting, etc. after you have combined all of the images.

Once you've made the adjustments to a single image, you need to apply them to all of the images you will be using to create the star trails. Make sure the image you've made the adjustments to is selected and then hit Ctrl+Shift+C (Cmd+Shift+C on a Mac). In the dialog box that appears, click on Check All and then click Copy. Now, go to the Library module and hit G to go into Grid View. Then, select all of the images you want to use (including the dark frame if you took one) and click Ctrl+Shift+V (Cmd+Shift+V on a Mac) to paste the settings onto all of the images. Alternatively, you can use the Auto Sync feature in Lightroom. However, I prefer not to use this. If you forget it is enabled, you might unintentionally make adjustments to multiple photos at once.

If you are exporting a very large number of images and/or have a slower computer, I recommend exporting the images as 8-bit TIFF files. Normally, I would recommend keeping the images at 16 bits. However, stacked star trail images can be so big that using 8 bits can keep the size down. On rare occasions, 8-bit files can produce banding in areas of the image with subtle gradations. If you notice this, you may want to go back and reprocess the images at 16 bits.

If there are any lights from planes or satellites in your images that you want to remove, I recommend doing this before you combine all of the images into star trails. You can do this in Lightroom before exporting the images or in Photoshop afterwards. I prefer using Photoshop since it has more cloning and healing brush options. Try not to clone out any of the bright stars, or that could create a gap in the star trails. You don't have to do a very precise job with this. Since this is just one of many layers that make up the image, any small imperfections in that layer will be much less noticeable in the final image. You should, however, check the final image to see if there are any problem areas.

You will now run the script made by Floris, using the instructions found on the download page. I recommend using the script that preserves the layers, so you can shorten the star trails afterwards if necessary. To shorten the star trails, just hide the first several layers and/or the last several layers in Photoshop.

If you took a dark frame, you can drag this onto the very top layer of your star trail image. Then just change the blending mode to Subtract.

After you run Floris's script, you should check the histogram of the resulting image in Photoshop. If there is a spike on the right side of the histogram, it means the highlights are blown out. You'll need to start over and push the exposure slider farther to the left on all of the images in Lightroom.

I produced this image of star trails over a remote arch in Arizona using a digital camera. I took 184 30-second exposures but only used 30 of the shots for this image. I created a comet-like effect with glowing heads using the Paint Daubs filter described in this chapter. Canon 5D II, 70mm, f2.8, 30 seconds, ISO 6400.

If you don't own Photoshop or aren't comfortable using scripts, there is an application called Startrails.exe created by Achim Schaller that you can download for free at http://www.startrails.de/html/software.html. I've found that this program creates very similar star trails to those produced by Floris's script. This software, however, doesn't give you the option of preserving the layers, so you'll have to reprocess the entire image if you want to make the star trails shorter. Also, you won't be able create special effects with this software, like the comet-like star trails described below.

Creating Comet-Like Star Trails

A lot of night photographers like altering the appearance of star trails so that they look like comets streaking across the sky. I personally don't like this effect as much, as I think it looks a little too unnatural. However, this can be a very eye-catching effect, and I would not discourage anyone from trying it. I'll first describe how to do this manually and then give links to some software that can do this for you.

Taking the Shots

If you want to create this effect, you'll need take a lot of consecutive shots with your digital camera, as described previously in this chapter. You'll need to avoid exposing the individuals images too long if you want to create a glowing head on the end of the star trail, like I did in the image on the previous page. You can use the rule of 2000 to calculate the maximum exposure time. If you're shooting with a 20mm lens, you'll take $2000/20 = 100$. So you would expose each shot for no more than 100 seconds. You can expose the images for shorter times if you want to produce brighter star trails. In this case, you can combine two or more of the exposures to create the glowing heads.

Manually Creating the Comet Trails

Once you've captured all of the images, you can combine them using Floris Van Breugel's script, as described in the previous section. Make sure to use the script that preserves the layers in Photoshop, not the one that flattens the image.

After you've created the star trail image, the first thing you need to do is change the opacity of all the layers so that they are progressively more opaque. This will create a tapering-off effect with the star trails. To do this, first take 100 divided by the number of layers in your image. For example, if there are 50 layers, you'll take $100/50 = 2$. You'll then want to change the very bottom layer to 2% opacity. This layer is the background layer, so to change its opacity, you'll first need to convert it to a regular layer by right-clicking on it and selecting Layer From Background... Next, change the opacity of the layer above this one to 4%, the layer above that to 6%, and so on until you get to the very top layer, which will remain at 100%.

You can change the direction of the tapering-off effect by starting with the top layer and moving down until you reach the bottom layer, which will remain at 100% opacity. I prefer to start with the bottom layer at 2%, as the stars will then appear to be moving in the same direction that they were in reality.

Once you've changed the opacity of the layers, you'll notice the tapering-off effect on the star trails. This effect alone is quite nice, and if you like it you may want to keep this as your final image. If you want to have a glowing head on the end of your star trail, there is a way to do this in Photoshop. After a lot of experimentation, the best result I achieved was with the Paint Daubs filter. This filter can be found by going to Filter > Filter Gallery... It only works with 8-bit files, so you'll need to convert your image to 8 bits if you are working with a 16-bit file.

First, you'll need to duplicate the top layer on your star trail image by right-clicking on it and selecting Duplicate Layer... Now, make sure the new, duplicate layer is selected and go to Filter > Artistic > Paint Daubs. I recommend using these settings:

Brush Size: 7 to 20
Sharpness: 0
Brush Type: Light Rough

Now, click Okay and you should see small glowing heads on the end of each star trail. This filter can blur the foreground, so you should mask out any foreground on this layer.

You can fine-tune the image and make the head glow more by selecting Filter > Blur > Gaussian Blur. You can try different radiuses and see what you like best. I recommend using a radius of 2-10 pixels.

Instead of creating the glowing head in Photoshop, you can produce it using a Photoshop plug-in called Star Spikes Pro. You'll again need to select the top, duplicate layer. To create a small glowing ball in Star Spikes Pro, you should keep the length of the spikes short and set the number of spikes to 32. This program is not available for Macs, but you can try using the Astronomy Tools Actions Set. These actions don't give you as much control over the appearance of the spikes, but they can produce interesting results.

You can also create the glowing head in-camera. Immediately after you are finished taking all of the shots for the star trails, you can take a single exposure with the stars out of focus. You can add this shot to the top layer of your star trail image and set the blending mode to Lighten.

StarStaX

If this sounds too difficult, there are software programs and Photoshop scripts that will do much of the work for you. The best free version I have found is StarStaX created by Markus Enzweiler at http://www.markus-enzweiler.de/software/software.html

To use this program, go to File > Open Images... and select all of the images you want to combine into star trails. If you took a dark frame, you can include this by going to File > Open Dark Frames...

Next, you can set your preferences by going to Edit > Preferences... I recommend setting the Blending Mode to Gap Filling. To create a comet effect, you should check the box next to Comet Mode. The slider below this allows you to select the length of the star trails. The middle setting seems to work well, but you can experiment with other settings. To make the comets appear to be moving in the opposite direction, check Process Images in Reverse Order. If you added a dark frame, select Subtract Dark Images. Now, go to Edit > Start Processing to create the star trails.

I've found that with the blending mode set to Gap Filling using the default settings, StarStaX creates images with a little more noticeable gaps than Floris's script or StarTrails.exe. You can reduce the gaps further by clicking on the wrench icon and adjusting the Threshold and Amount sliders. However, this can also widen the star trails and make them start to overlap with neighboring star trails. Also, it can cause the highlights to be blown out on some of the brighter star trails. I therefore still prefer Floris's script and StarTrails.exe. The difference will likely only be noticeable in larger prints, though, so this program can be useful for the ease of creating the comet effect.

StarStaX does not allow you to create the glowing heads at the end of the star trails, and it doesn't preserve the layers to allow you to do this yourself. You can manually add this layer in Photoshop by dragging the last image that was used in creating the star trails onto the image created by StarStaX. Then, set the blending mode to Lighten, and create the glowing head as described in the previous section.

Sam Waguila's Script

There is a Photoshop script created by Sam Waguila that will create the comet effect and a separate layer for creating the glowing head. It also has several other creative options for creating star trails. Unfortunately, this script creates noticeable gaps in the star trails. I therefore don't recommend it for images that you'll be printing. However, if you're only preparing the images for web presentation, the gaps won't likely be noticeable. The script can be downloaded for free at http://www.waguilaphotography.com/1/post/2013/09/waguila_startrail_stacker-script.html

Advanced Stacker Plus

A more robust set of actions for creating special effects with star trails was created by Steven Christenson. It costs $41.99, but you can get a stripped-down trial version that creates small watermarked images. As with Sam Waguila's script, these actions create noticeable gaps in the star trails. I've heard that Steven may try to fix this in future versions. For now, though, the paid version is probably only suitable for those who really enjoy creating different effects with star trails and plan to use them mainly for web presentation. These actions can be purchased at http://starcircleacademy.com/getstacking/.

Moon Trails

One interesting thing you can do with star trails is to also include the moon in the shot. This will create a much wider trail in the sky. I recommend shooting moon trails under a moon that is just 4%-12% illuminated. If the moon is any less illuminated, it will set

This image shows the moon, Venus, and Jupiter (all on the left side) streaking above the Three Gossips in Arches National Park. I took this shot when the moon was only 9% illuminated. As a result, it appeared as a fairly slender line, rather than a large blob. I did a single 40-minute exposure on a digital camera so as to avoid having the moon trail become too wide and bright. I also wanted the two planets to stand out and not have other bright star trails competing with them. Canon 5D II, 35mm, f4.0, 40 minutes, ISO 100.

in the evening before it's dark enough to photograph a moon trail (or it will rise too late in the morning). If the moon is more than 12% illuminated, it will start to look like a wide blob and can drown out nearby stars. It is, however, still possible to get some interesting results under a brighter moon, so you can experiment with this.

Just like star trails, you can shoot moon trails with a long, single exposure or by combining multiple exposures on a digital camera. This is one situation where a single exposure can be advantageous. The moon is bright enough that you may prefer the fainter trails from a long exposure. Also, the dark noise will not be as bad as it would be under no moon. You should, however, still use Long Exposure Noise Reduction.

You can also use a film camera to capture moon trails. However, since you can get good results with a digital camera, I don't personally find this necessary. Determining the proper exposure can be tricky with film, since you can't take a test shot. The moon can vary in brightness significantly depending on what phase it is in. I recommend shooting under a thin crescent moon and using an aperture between f4.0 and f6.7 to avoid overexposing the image.

VIII. Stitching Images

Even if you have some of the best camera equipment for night photography and you properly expose all of your photographs, you'll still find that there is a fair amount of noise in the images. This noise may not be very apparent when an image is seen at small sizes. However, if you want to make a large print of the image, the noise can become more problematic. One of the best solutions I've found for this is to create large stitched images.

A stitched image is one where you take multiple shots, each comprising a small part of the scene you want to photograph. You later use computer software to "stitch" each of these images together to produce an image of the whole scene. Since you're stitching together multiple images, the resulting file will be much larger than one from a single shot. There will still be noise in the image, but since the file size is so much larger, you have to zoom in much farther to actually see the noise. You can therefore print the image at much larger sizes before the noise becomes noticeable.

Another advantage of a stitched image is that there is no limit to how wide your image can be. You can do a full 360-degree panoramic photo with a stitched image, something that is impossible with a single shot. This is important because some things you photograph at night, like the Milky Way or the northern lights, cover a large portion of the sky.

EQUIPMENT

You don't usually need specialized equipment to create stitched images. However, if you'll be doing a lot of stitched images, there are some items that can make stitching a little easier.

Tripod Head

When taking stitched images, some photographers use panoramic tripod heads. These tripod heads keep the entrance pupil of the lens at a fixed spot as you turn the camera. This is important because it will prevent any parallax error in the images. This means that, as you turn the camera, objects in the image will appear in the same relative positions in each shot you take. This makes it easier for the stitching software to seamlessly stitch all of the images together.

I have found that panoramic tripod heads are not usually necessary for stitching images taken at night. You have limited depth of field when taking shots at night, especially with the longer lenses that you will use for stitching images. You will therefore need to avoid including close foreground subjects in the shot when shooting stitched images. Parallax is much less noticeable when you don't have close foreground objects. Furthermore, stitching software has improved so much in recent years that it can still create seamless images even if there is some noticeable parallax.

A panoramic tripod head might be helpful if you are stitching together images using an ultra-wide lens that can provide more depth of field and you are including objects closer than 10 feet to you in the foreground. Another time it can be useful is if you have a close foreground and are focus stacking each of the individual shots to increase the depth of field. However, focus stacking and then stitching images is a complicated task, and I only recommend it for those who are very proficient in photography and post-processing.

If you don't currently own a panoramic tripod head but are considering purchasing one, I recommend first using your current tripod head to stitch images at night. You may be surprised at how rare the circumstances are when you really need a panoramic head.

One thing that can be helpful when creating stitched images is a tripod head with degree markings on it. The markings will show you how many degrees you have turned the camera between each shot. This will help ensure that you leave plenty of overlap between

Left: Clouds float above Arenal Volcano in Costa Rica. I stitched together three horizontal images to help reduce noise from the now-outdated camera I used. Canon 5D, 35mm, f1.6, 15 seconds, ISO 1600.

each of the images so that they can be stitched together without gaps.

3-way pan/tilt heads (not to be confused with panoramic heads) are a little better for stitching images than ball heads. However, as long your ball head has a rotating base, I've found it fairly easy to create them with either tripod head. If your ball head doesn't have a rotating base, you will need to make sure your camera remains level as you turn it. This isn't too difficult with small stitched images, but it can be very tricky to do with large stitched images.

The Acratech Ultimate Ballhead and the Manfrotto 498RC2 that I recommended in Chapter I do have degree markings and rotating bases.

Leveling Base

Another optional item you can buy is a leveling base, which is mounted between the tripod and tripod head. It will ensure that your tripod head is mounted on a perfectly level surface. This is important because as you turn your tripod head horizontally, it will remain level and you won't have to adjust the leveling after every image you take.

If your tripod has a bubble level on top of its legs, you can use this instead of a leveling base. You just need to adjust the tripod legs until the bubble is centered in the level. If you don't have a bubble level on your tripod legs, you can remove your tripod head and place a bubble level on top of the legs where the tripod head would be. You can then adjust the legs until the bubble is centered from all angles. Leveling the tripod legs can be a somewhat tedious task, so if you do a large number of stitched images, a leveling base might be a worthwhile investment. However, I don't recommend purchasing one if you are just starting out doing stitched images.

Lenses

As I mentioned in Chapter I, I recommend using a 35mm or 50mm lens with a wide aperture for most of your stitched images. These lenses capture a smaller portion of the scene than wide angle lenses, so you will need to take more shots to create a stitched image of the entire scene. This is a good thing because the more images you stitch together, the larger the resulting photo will be. The larger the photo is, the larger

you will be able to print it before it has noticeable amounts of noise.

If you want to include a close foreground object in your stitched image, you may need to use a wider lens in order to expand the depth of field and get everything in focus. You can refer to page 57 to see how much depth of field you can achieve with common lenses and aperture settings.

Another time you may want to use a wider lens is if there is something moving in the scene, like clouds or the northern lights. You will want to take fewer images so that the objects move as little as possible during the time it takes you to capture all of the shots. If the objects move too much, the stitching software may have a difficult time seamlessly stitching all of the images together.

Wider lenses do produce more distortion in each image, which can make it more difficult to stitch the images together. Fortunately, stitching software has improved to the point where this is no longer as big of an issue. I've found that you can usually stitch together single-row panoramas using lenses as wide as 14mm on a full-frame camera. The only lens you really don't want to use when stitching images together is a fisheye lens, as the distortion produced by these lenses is too extreme.

Robotic Camera Mounts

GigaPan produces the EPIC Pro Robotic Camera Mount that can automatically take all of the shots for a stitched image. I would only consider this device if you plan to create a very large number of stitched images. It weighs over seven pounds, making it a little cumbersome if you plan to hike with it. Also, it takes about 15 minutes to set up, by which time you could have already manually taken a fairly large stitched image.

A robotic mount is more useful if you are using a long telephoto lens to capture hundreds or thousands of images to stitch together. This would be difficult and tedious to do manually. However, a long telephoto lens isn't very practical for stitching nightscape images, as the stars will move too much relative to the foreground during the time it takes to capture all of the images. The longest lens I would recommend using is 85mm.

This image shows the northern lights over a lake near Yellowknife, Canada. Since the aurora spanned over half the sky, my 14mm lens was not wide enough to capture the entire scene. However, the northern lights were moving too fast for me to do a large stitched image. So I shot a single row of six vertical images using my 14mm lens. I used a short shutter speed to minimize movement of the aurora, and I shot all six images as fast as I could. The resulting image is 82 megapixels. Nikon D800e, 14mm, f2.8, 13 seconds, ISO 6400.

CAMERA SETTINGS

Stitched images can be taken with any digital SLR camera. You need to make sure to use the exact same settings for every shot you take. To do this, you'll have to set your camera to manual mode (though you'll almost always have it in manual mode when shooting at night anyway).

I generally use the rule of 500 when determining shutter speeds for stitched images. If I'm using a 50mm lens to shoot the images, I'll take 500 / 50 = 10 seconds per exposure. This may seem counterintuitive because the final image is going to have a much wider field of view than a 50mm lens. It may be closer to the field of view from a 14mm lens. So you might think that you should use the same shutter speeds you would with a 14mm lens. Using the rule of 500, this would be 500/14 = 35 seconds. However, at 35 seconds you can start to see star tails in the very large prints that are made possible by stitched images. I therefore find that using the rule of 500 with the focal length of the lens that I'm using to take the shots works well.

Another advantage of these shorter exposures is that the stars won't move as much in the sky while you are taking the shots. The software will then have an easier time stitching everything together.

If there is something in the scene that is moving fairly quickly, like clouds or the northern lights, I'll sometimes use even shorter shutter speeds than the rule of 500 would suggest. This helps minimize movement between exposures.

For the aperture and ISO, you can usually use the same settings as those described in Chapter IV. One exception to this is that you can sometimes get away with apertures wider than f1.6. There will likely be a lot of coma in the corners of these images. However, you can get around this by cropping off the edges of the images, as I will describe later.

TAKING THE PHOTOS

Once you have your camera settings dialed in, you just need to take all of the images. Make sure your tripod head is mounted on a level surface by adjusting your tripod legs or by using a leveling base. If you want to ensure that your tripod head is mounted properly, you can turn it horizontally and see if the bubble level on your tripod head or camera remains centered.

Before beginning the stitched image, I recommend taking a test shot. Point your camera towards the brightest part of the scene you will be photographing and take an image using the camera settings you have decided on. Once you've taken the shot, check the histogram to make sure you are not overexposing the image. If you are, lower the ISO until you are not clipping the highlights. You'll also want to zoom in on your shot and make sure everything is in sharp focus. If you have a close foreground in your image, you'll want to take a test shot of the nearest foreground and a test shot of the sky using the same focus settings. Make sure that both the foreground and background are in sharp focus.

If everything looks okay, you can start taking your stitched image. Ideally, you'll want to use a remote shutter release for all of your shots to avoid camera shake. If you don't have one, I recommend using a two-second self-timer on your camera if it has one.

Make sure you have Long Exposure Noise Reduction turned off, as it will take too long between each shot. If you want, you can take a single dark frame, which you can later subtract from all of the images before stitching them. However, stitched images are usually of such high quality and dark noise is so low with shorter exposures that I don't find this necessary.

You will want to position your camera to take an image of the far bottom corner of the scene. If you start at the far bottom left, I recommend framing the image a little bit to the left and below the scene you want to photograph. This will give you some breathing room to ensure that you capture every part of the scene. It is easy to later crop out parts of the scene you don't want to include in the final image.

I recommend shooting all shots horizontally, even if you final image will be vertical. The camera is steadier when it is mounted horizontally, and it is easier to operate. Also, the entrance pupil of the lens will move less from shot to shot, making it easier to stitch the images if you have a close foreground. One exception to this is if you are just taking one row of vertical images. This can be easier than taking two rows of horizontal images.

You will need to make sure that your camera is level using a bubble level or your camera's built-in leveling feature. You can now take the first shot. After you take this shot, you'll need to rotate your camera to the right before taking the second shot. Make sure to only rotate the camera horizontally, and don't change the tilt of the camera or the vertical angle. You can do this even with a ball head, as long as it has a rotating base. Just make sure to keep the ball itself tight and

rotate the base of the tripod head.

You'll need to leave plenty of overlap between the images. This will make it easier for the software to stitch the images, and it will ensure that there are no gaps in the image. You can determine the exact amount to rotate the camera using a formula I've come up with that I will call the 750 method. I'll call it a method so as not to confuse it with the rule of 500 that is used to calculate shutter speed. For the 750 method, take 750 divided by the focal length of your lens to determine the number of degrees that you should rotate your camera between each shot. For example, if you are using a 50mm lens you take 750/50=15. You should rotate your camera 15 degrees between each shot. If you don't have a full-frame camera, you'll need to first multiply the focal length of the lens by the crop factor of the camera. The 750 method will leave a lot of overlap between each image. If you are in a hurry or don't want to take so many images, you can bump this up to the 1000 method, which will allow you to turn the camera a little farther between each shot.

The 750 method will only work if your tripod head has degree markings on it, so you know how much you are rotating the camera. If it doesn't have degree markings, you'll just need to make sure and leave plenty of overlap between each image you take.

Now that you know how far to rotate the camera, just take a shot, quickly rotate the camera the right amount, take another shot, rotate the camera, and so on until you've captured the entire field of view that you want to capture. Again, I recommend erring on the side of caution and capturing more of the scene than you want in your final image.

If you're only taking a single-row panorama, then you will be done once you've rotated the camera all the way to the right side of the scene. However, since the sky is so large, you will often need to do multi-row panoramas, especially if you aren't using a wide angle lens. When you get to the end of the first row, you'll need to rotate your camera up. If you have a panoramic head or a 3-way pan/tilt head with vertical degree markings, you can use this. You can use the 750 method to determine how much to rotate the camera up. If you don't have vertical degree markings, you should just try to rotate the camera up about half of the vertical field of view of your camera. You can compare the image you take to the previous one to make sure you can see some of the same stars in

---

When I took this shot, the northern lights covered most of the sky in northern Alaska. I therefore spun around in circles for over an hour in sub-zero temperatures, taking numerous 360-degree panoramas. I later picked out this one as my favorite. Canon 5D II, 14mm, f2.8, 8 seconds, ISO 6400, eight images stitched together.

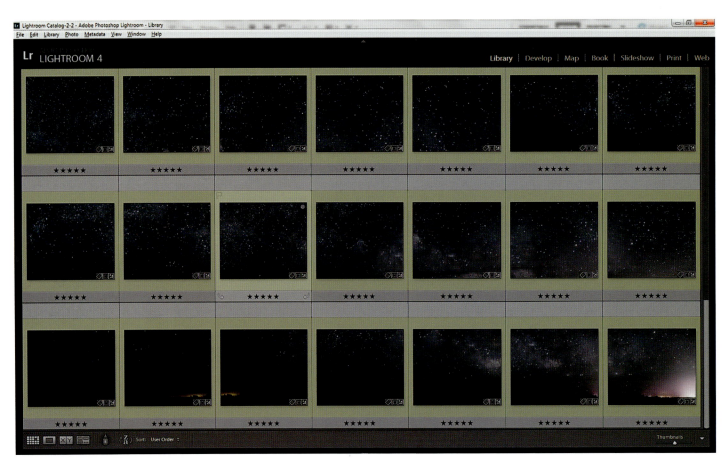

This Lightroom screenshot shows all 21 photos I took of the Milky Way over Balanced Rock in Arches National Park. I processed each of the images with the exact same settings in Lightroom. I checked the box next to Enable Profile Corrections to remove some of the vignetting in the corners, which could have made it more difficult for the software to stitch the images seamlessly. I also cropped off the left and right sides of all the images, as this is where the lens performs the worst and can produce coma in the corners. This can be especially problematic with the ultra-wide aperture of f1.2 that I was using.

---

each image. If you're using a ball head, you may inadvertently tilt the camera while rotating it upwards. So make sure the camera is level before starting your next row of images.

Now, you'll just need to take images and rotate the camera to the left until you've reached the far left side of the scene. Then, rotate the camera up again and take another row of images. Repeat this process until you've photographed all of the scene you want to capture. This process may sound complicated, but it's actually fairly simple once you get the hang of it. You will want to take all of the images as fast as you can, as the stars will be moving while you take the images. If the stars move too much during the time it takes to capture all of the images, it may be difficult for the software to stitch the images together. However, stitching software has improved so much that it will normally be able align all the stars and create a seamless image.

PROCESSING THE IMAGES IN LIGHTROOM

Once you've taken all the shots, you can import them into Lightroom. You will initially want to process just one of the images, preferably one that includes the brightest part of the scene that you photographed.

I recommend first cropping off the left and right sides of the image to make it nearly square. This will help eliminate any coma that is in the corners of your image. Cropping the corners will also help to minimize vignetting and distortion, both of which can make stitching images together more difficult. If you used the 750 method, there will still be plenty of overlap between the images to be able to stitch them all together. If for any reason your stitching software has trouble combining the images, you can go back and

VIII. Stitching Images

By stitching together the images seen on the previous page, I was able to create this seamless photo of the entire scene. I then optimized the image in Photoshop to bring out more contrast and colors, including the green colors created by airglow. Canon 5D II, 50mm, f1.2, 15 seconds, ISO 6400.

---

crop off less of the sides. However, I have never encountered a problem with this.

You can now adjust some of the sliders in the Develop module. You don't have to get anything perfect, as you can always adjust things further in Photoshop after you've stitched all of the images together. The most important sliders to adjust for stitched images are the Highlights and Shadows and those in the Lens Corrections panel. I'll therefore describe them in more detail here. Other sliders that I frequently use are discussed in Chapter X.

If you're clipping the highlights, you should move the Highlights slider to the left until they are not clipped. This is the reason I suggest working on an image of the brightest part of the scene. If you make sure this part isn't clipped, you can be confident nothing else will be clipped.

If you want to bring out any detail in the shadows, you can push the Shadows slider to the right. Be aware, though, that this will also bring out extra noise in the image. Sometimes you're better off leaving dark areas as silhouettes. If there's a specific part of the scene where you want to bring out detail in the shadows, you can select an image that contains that part of the scene and see how much of a Shadows adjustment is necessary. Then, go back to the main image you're working on and move the Shadows slider the same amount.

In the Lens Correction panel, you can go to Profile and click on Enable Profile Corrections. This will help eliminate distortion and vignetting, which will make it easier to stitch the images together. If the image still doesn't look good, you can fine tune things using the Distortion and Vignetting sliders. If your lens profile is not found and you weren't able to select Enable Profile Corrections, you can click on Manual and adjust the sliders there.

Once you've made the adjustments to a single image, you need to apply them to all of the images you plan to stitch together. Make sure the image you've made the adjustments to is selected and then hit Ctrl+Shift+C (Cmd+Shift+C on a Mac). In the dialog box that appears, click on Check All and then click Copy. Now, go to the Library module and hit G to go into Grid View. Then, select all of the images you want to stitch and click Ctrl+Shift+V (Cmd+Shift+V on a Mac) to paste the settings onto all of the images.

You can now export all of the images by selecting them and hitting Ctrl+Shift+E (Cmd+Shift+E on a Mac). If you have a slower computer that may have problems with really large files, you can export the images as 8-bit TIFF files in order to keep the size down. If you're doing a smaller stitched image or you have a powerful computer that can easily handle huge files, you can keep the images at 16 bits. This will preserve all of the color data in your image.

STITCHING SOFTWARE

Once you've exported all of the images, you'll need to combine them using stitching software. I'll discuss the pros and cons of some of the most popular software below.

Photoshop

For a long time, Photoshop did a rather poor job stitching images. However, Photoshop has steadily improved, and it can now do a very good job with most images. Occasionally, it does still have difficulty stitching together very large photos. It can also be rather slow when attempting to stitch large images, even with a fast computer.

To stitch images in Photoshop, go to File > Automate > Photomerge. In the screen that pops up, I recommend leaving the Layout set to Auto. You can keep Blend Images Together selected and leave the other

In this image, Mount Baldy is illuminated in a pond at Paradise Divide in Colorado. I timed this shot so that the quarter moon would be behind me and illuminating the front of the mountain. I took 30 photos and stitched them together to create a 200 megapixel image. Canon 5D II, 50mm, f1.8, 13 seconds, ISO 6400.

boxes unchecked. Then, browse for the images you want to stitch and click OK.

If Photoshop fails to stitch the images together or the stitch doesn't look very good, you can try clicking Vignette Removal and/or Geometric Distortion Correction in the Photomerge dialog box. With Geometric Distortion Correction, Photoshop can sometimes do a good job stitching a small number of images taken with an ultra-wide angle lens. Vignette Removal can help if there is noticeable darkening around the edges of the individual images (though it's better if you were able to minimize this in Lightroom).

Microsoft Image Composite Editor (ICE)

This is a great program for stitching images that is available for free for non-commercial use at http://research.microsoft.com/projects/ice/. I've experienced few problems with ICE in the tests I've done on some of my images. It does an especially good job with very large stitched images, and it is relatively fast when creating a preview of these images. I have experienced some problems when attempting to stitch images taken with very wide angle lenses. Since this program is made by Microsoft, it is only available for PCs.

To use Microsoft Ice, click Ctrl+N to create a new panorama. Then select all the images you want to stitch and click Open. If it is able to stitch the images, it will show a preview of the stitched image.

For most stitched images, it should let you click on the small cube at the top of the program. You can then change the Projection options until you get a result that you like best. On this screen, it will also let you adjust the distortion of the image by clicking and dragging the image up and down or left to right (though the left to right option usually only works with single-row panoramas). This can be especially useful if the horizon appears curved, and you need to straighten it. Click Apply when you are done making adjustments in this screen.

This image shows the Milky Way rising above rock formations in the Garden of Eden in Arches National Park. I used Stellarium to find out when the Milky Way would be rising over these formations. I then took 70 images of the scene to create a 450 megapixel photo. Canon 5D II, 50mm, f1.2, 10 seconds, ISO 6400.

If the image looks good to you, select the format you want for the exported image. I recommend using TIFF Image or Adobe Photoshop. If you select Photoshop, it will give you the option of exporting it Flat or with Layers. I recommend selecting Flat. Now click on Export to Disk... to save the image.

Hugin

Hugin is a free panorama stitching software that can be used with a Mac as well as a PC. It does a good job with most images but can be very slow with large images. It's fairly simple to use. First, click on Load images... and select the images you want to stitch. Then, click Align..., and it will try to stitch the images. If it's successful, the resulting image will show up on the screen.

You may need to click on the Crop tab and adjust the crop, as it can crop the image a little too tight. You can also adjust the appearance of the stitch by clicking on the Projection panel. Usually, the default option will work best. If the horizon appears curved or the image appears distorted, you can adjust it by clicking on the Move/Drag tab and using the Straighten tool. There are also some more advanced options in this program, but you normally won't need them.

Once the image looks good to you, you can return to the Assistant panel and click Create Panorama... to save the file.

Auto Pano Pro

This used to be the program of choice for many pho-

tographers who created stitched images. However, other software programs have nearly caught up to it and seem to do just as good of a job with most images. If you find that the other programs I've mentioned are unable to stitch together an image, you can use the free trail of Auto Pano Pro. If it is able to stitch the image, you could consider buying the software, since the trial version only creates watermarked images. This software sells for around $130 and can be purchased at http://www.kolor.com/.

PT Gui

PT Gui is a stitching program you can purchase for a little over $100 at http://www.ptgui.com/. Like Auto Pano Pro, you can use the trial version of this software if you're having difficulty stitching an image with other programs.

PROCESSING THE IMAGES IN PHOTOSHOP

Once you've stitched all of the images together, you can open the resulting file in Photoshop. The first thing you should do is zoom all the way in to make sure you have a seamless stitch. If you find any issues, they can usually be fixed with a healing brush. You can now work on the image like you would any other image in Photoshop. I will discuss post-processing techniques I use on night photos in Chapter X.

When you start adding new layers to your image, it can increase the file size considerably. This shouldn't be a problem if you have a fast computer with a lot of RAM and a solid state drive. If you don't, it can cause your computer to slow to a crawl. If this happens, you can flatten the image and save it with a new name. This isn't an ideal workflow for processing images in Photoshop, as it's better to use a non-destructive workflow and keep all of the layers intact. However, this can become impractical with really large images. As long as you save the file with a new name, you can always go back to the original file if necessary.

IX. Blending Multiple Exposures

Even if you use all of the techniques described so far, there will still be situations where it can be difficult to capture great night photos.

If you want to photograph a vast, sweeping landscape at night that has both a near foreground and a very distant background, it is nearly impossible to evenly illuminate the entire scene with a flashlight. Sometimes you can time the photograph so that there is a crescent moon behind you that can illuminate the scene. However, there are situations when even this will not work.

If you are shooting from inside an alcove or rock cave, the moon will never be able to fully illuminate the inside of it. If you are photographing a deep canyon or have a mountain or cliff face behind you, the moon may only be able to illuminate the scene when it is high in the sky. When the moon is too high, it can produce harsh lighting, just like the sun does during the day. Also, if you want to capture a detailed and dramatic image of the Milky Way, even a crescent moon can obscure the stars too much to capture the image you want.

Another time you may have difficulty shooting night photos is if you're trying to photograph a constellation, but the camera captures so many stars that the constellation is not recognizable in the image. There will also be times when you can't get enough depth of field in a single exposure to get the foreground and background of your image in focus.

In situations like these, your best option may be to take two or more different exposures of the scene and blend them together in post-processing.

Blending multiple exposures can be a difficult thing to do well and often requires a lot of skill in Photoshop. When done properly, it can be a very valuable skill for a night photographer. When done improperly, it can be a way to create some truly hideous images! So I recommend becoming proficient in other techniques in this book before attempting to blend multiple exposures.

There are many software programs, including Nik's HDR Efex Pro, which can blend multiple exposures to create high dynamic range (HDR) images for you. For night photos, this will likely not be useful for all situations where you want to blend exposures. Some situations require more specialized techniques. I therefore recommend learning how to do this manually in Photoshop. This will give you the most control over how you want the final image to appear.

If blending multiple exposures sounds too daunting to you, I will first discuss a way to mimic the effect of blending two exposures with a single shot.

BLACK CARD TECHNIQUE

The black card technique (sometimes referred to as the magic cloth) allows you to mimic the effect of a graduated neutral density filter. This filter is dark on one half and light on the other, and it can be used if one part of the scene is significantly brighter than the other. You can hold the filter up against your lens so that the dark part of it blocks the light from the brighter part of the scene. This will even out the amount of light that hits the sensor and prevent you from overexposing or underexposing part of the shot.

As mentioned in Chapter I, it's not very practical to use filters like this at night. Since there is so little light to work with, you don't want a filter to block

---

Left: The Milky Way rises above canyons carved out by the Green River in Canyonlands National Park. To create this image, I took a shot of the land shortly after sunset and captured a stitched image of the sky an hour after sunset. I then blended the two images in Photoshop. Nikon D800e; exposure of land: 14mm, f8.0, 15 seconds, ISO 100; exposures of sky: 50mm, f1.8, 10 seconds, ISO 6400, 28 images stitched together.

out even more light. This can significantly increase the amount of noise in your image. If you try to compensate for this by doing longer exposures to let in more light, the stars will begin to appear as small star trails rather than as points of light.

An alternative to this is to block some of the light from the sky from entering your camera lens using a black card, mouse pad, glove or cloth. This allows you to expose the sky for a shorter amount of time than the rest of the scene. This will prevent you from getting short star trails in the sky and will allow you to expose the foreground longer.

You will generally want to use the black card technique when the foreground of your image is noticeably darker than the night sky. This can occur near the end of twilight on a moonless night, when just a little bit of light is illuminating the foreground. It can also occur after twilight when only a sliver of the moon is illuminating the foreground. If a brighter moon is out, the foreground should be bright enough relative to the sky that you won't need the black card.

Another situation in which you may be able to use the black card is when no moon is out, but you have a very bright and reflective foreground, like snow, ice, or a reflective surface like a lake.

If no moon is out and you have a darker foreground, the disparity in the brightness of the sky and land may be too extreme to successfully use a black card. In this case, you will likely have to blend multiple exposures, as will be discussed later in this chapter.

To use the black card technique, you'll first want to calculate what your exposure time would be with the rule of 500. If you're using a 20mm lens, take 500/20 = 25. The exposure time would be 25 seconds. This is how long you'll want to expose the sky in your image. When you take the shot, wait 25 seconds and then cover the top part of your lens with the card or cloth so that it blocks out the light from the sky. It may take some practice to block just the right part of the lens. You'll want to slowly move the card or cloth up and down just a fraction of an inch during the exposure. This will help prevent a hard and obvious transition between the part of the scene that is covered by the card or cloth and the part that isn't covered.

You can continue exposing the bottom part of the scene as long as necessary to get a good, balanced exposure of the entire scene. After you take the shot, be sure to review it carefully on your LCD screen. Make sure you were holding the card in the right position so that it was covering just the sky. Also, make sure that the brightness of the sky and foreground match and that one isn't significantly brighter than the other. If you see any issues, you'll need to make adjustments and try another shot until you get an image you like.

When using the black card technique, you may benefit from using a dark frame or your camera's Long Exposure Noise Reduction. With longer exposures in such low light, dark noise can become more noticeable.

Shots taken with the black card usually work best when there is a flat horizon where the sky meets the land. If there are curved rock formations or mountains jutting into the sky, it will be difficult to get an evenly illuminated image using the black card. In this case, you may need to blend two different exposures, as I'll describe next.

MULTIPLE SHOTS AT ONE TIME

Instead of using a black card, you can take two different exposures - one for the land and one for the sky. As with the black card, this may be necessary when the foreground isn't completely dark but is noticeably darker than the sky.

Unlike the black card technique, you can also do this when the land and sky are more evenly illuminated. Although you can get a good exposure with a single shot under these conditions, blending two exposures can result in a higher quality image. This is because you'll be able to take longer exposures of the land with a lower ISO, which will result in an image with less noise. The shot of the sky may then appear noisier than the shot of the land. You can compensate for this when doing noise reduction in post-processing. Since the sky doesn't have as much detail as the land, you can be more aggressive with noise reduction on the sky without worrying about blurring the details.

I took this image of False Kiva shortly after sunset. It would have been way too dark to capture detail inside the alcove at night without a flashlight. Canon 5D II, 14mm, f8.0, 1.6 seconds, ISO 100.

I captured this image of the Milky Way above False Kiva a little over an hour later from the exact same spot. Canon 5D II, 14mm, f2.8, 30 seconds, ISO 6400.

To capture these images, you first want to take an exposure for the sky using the rule of 500 and the camera settings outlined in Chapter IV. For the shot of the land, I recommend exposures of 2-4 minutes. Longer exposures can show too much dark noise, and shorter exposures can have more photon noise. This exposure length seems to strike a good balance between the two and can give you better quality images. If you overexpose the shot with these longer exposures, you'll need to reduce the ISO. However, you only need to worry about overexposing the land. It doesn't matter if you overexpose the sky, as you won't be using that part of the image.

As with the black card technique, you may benefit from using a dark frame or your camera's Long Exposure Noise Reduction. You may only need to use the dark frame on the longer exposure for the land, as this is where dark noise becomes more noticeable.

To blend the two images, you can open both of them in Photoshop. Then, select the Move tool, hold down the Shift key, and drag the image with the exposure for the sky onto the other photo. The image you drag it onto will then have two layers - the top one with the exposure for the sky and the bottom one with the exposure for the land.

You should select both layers and click Edit > Auto-Align Layers... You can keep the default setting at Auto and click OK. This step isn't always necessary and may not work if the images are too different from one another. However, even if you took the two images from the same spot, they may be slightly misaligned, especially if you changed the focus between the two shots.

You'll now need to select only the sky in the top layer. The easiest way to do this is usually with the Quick Select Tool. Once you've selected the sky, you'll need to make a mask on the top layer. You can do this by selecting the top layer and clicking on the rectangular icon with a circle in the middle of it at the bottom of the Layers panel. It will then mask out everything except the sky. The land from the layer below this one will show through, and you'll have combined the two images.

If the mask you create isn't perfect, you can refine it by right-clicking on the mask and selecting Refine Edge... The Edge Detection feature in the dialog box is one of the more useful options for refining the mask. To use this, you have to check the box next to Smart Radius and then adjust the radius until you get a result you like. This feature can be especially useful for areas of the sky that are difficult to select, like those where tree branches are silhouetted against the sky.

You can also experiment with other sliders in this panel. The Feather slider will mimic the effect of a

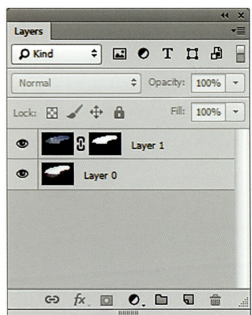

I combined the two exposures on the previous page by dragging the right image onto the left one. I then selected the sky on the top layer and masked out everything else, as can be seen in the Layers panel above. The resulting image is comprised of the land from the bottom layer and the sky from the top layer. As you can see, the blend is not perfect, especially where the distant land meets the sky. This is a common problem when blending two exposures taken at different times.

---

graduated-neutral density filter by creating a more gradual transition between the exposure for the land and the exposure for the sky. This slider will likely only work if the two images you are blending are fairly similar to begin with. Otherwise, it can create too much of a halo along the edges.

If you still can't get a natural-looking result after refining the mask, you may have to use a clone brush or a healing brush on areas of the image that are close to the edge of the mask to try and create a more natural blend.

You'll also want to individually adjust the contrast and brightness of both layers until they better match each other. You can use techniques described in the Photoshop Adjustments section of Chapter X to fine tune the image. This is as much of an art form as it is a science. You just need to work on the image until you get a result that you like.

MULTIPLE SHOTS AT DIFFERENT TIMES

If you're shooting with no moon out and don't have a very bright or reflective foreground, blending multiple exposures as described in the previous section will not likely work as well. When it gets dark enough to capture dramatic images of the night sky, the foreground may be so dark that you cannot get very good detail with low noise levels even by increasing the exposure time.

One solution to this is to take the two exposures at different times. You can take an exposure for the foreground during civil twilight, when it is still light enough to capture a lot of detail in the land. I recommend taking this shot about 5-10 minutes after sunset. At this time, you should still be able to use your camera's exposure meter to determine the proper exposure. Also, if you have close foreground objects, it will still be bright enough to use smaller apertures and get more depth of field.

You'll now need to wait until it gets dark. Make sure and leave your camera and tripod at the same spot. You can take the second exposure for the sky during or after astronomical twilight.

If you'll be shooting the two exposures in the morning rather than the evening, you'll just need to take the exposures in the opposite order I described.

You'll later need to blend the two photos in post-processing. You can use the same method as described in the previous section. It is more difficult to blend these exposures than two shots taken one after the other. This is because the light on the scene will be different at the times you take the two shots. For the white balance, you'll likely need to use a lower color temperature for the exposure of the sky than for the exposure of the land. Also, at any point where the land meets the sky in the image, you'll usually want the land to appear darker than the sky. Images where too much of the land appears lighter than the sky can look very unnatural. To achieve this result, you'll need to gradually darken the land as it approaches the horizon. The Burn/Dodge layer described in Chapter X can be useful for this. You will likely also want to do several other adjustments described in this chapter to achieve a satisfactory result.

BLENDING STITCHED IMAGES

If you blend two exposures taken at different times as described in the previous section, you will likely find that the sky has quite a bit more noise than the land. This is because the shot of the sky was taken when it was much darker out. This likely won't be a problem when the image is viewed at small sizes. However, if you want to make a large print of the image, it can look unnatural to have more detail and better quality in one part of the image than the other.

I refined the image on the previous page by using a Burn/Dodge Layer in Photoshop to darken the land near the horizon so it did not appear lighter than the sky. I also used Tony Kuyper's luminosity masks to bring out some more detail in the shadows and increase contrast in the sky. I then adjusted the colors and saturation in the sky and land until I got a result that looked good to me. Several of the techniques I used will be described in more detail in the next chapter.

Although the image of False Kiva on the previous page turned out well, the sky is too noisy to print at very large sizes. To overcome this problem in this image, I stitched together multiple images of the rock formations taken shortly after sunset and blended them with a large stitched image of the night sky taken during astronomical twilight before sunrise. Canon 5D II; exposures of land: 24mm, f16, 0.6 seconds, ISO 100; exposures of sky: 50mm, f1.8, 13 seconds, ISO 6400.

A solution I've found to this problem is to take a large stitched image of the sky using a 35mm or 50mm lens. You can then blend this photo with a single exposure of the land. You will first need to up-res the exposure of the land so that it matches the size of the larger stitched image of the sky. To do this, I recommend using the Preserve Details (enlargement) option in the Image Size dialog box in Photoshop CC.

Even after you up-res the shot of the land, the two images won't line up perfectly. However, you can still blend the photos with some extra work in Photoshop. If necessary, you can distort one or both of the images a little to line them up better. You can also do some cloning to fix any areas where they don't line up well. It can, however, be very difficult and tedious to do this and get natural-looking photographs. It is therefore only suitable for those who are very proficient in Photoshop. I will usually only use this technique if I have an image in mind that I think can be very dramatic and is worth the time involved.

I should note that instead of taking just one stitched image, you can take two stitched images with the same lens for both the land and the sky. I've done this for a couple of images. However, I've found that they don't tend to line up any better when you combine them. This is because the stitching software can distort each of the images in different ways. I've also found that the quality of a single exposure of the land pretty closely matches the quality of a large stitched image of the sky. So you really don't need the extra resolution and detail that you get from a stitched image of the land. Since it's easier not to do this stitched image, using a single exposure for the land has become my preferred method.

One exception to this is if the scene I am photographing is so wide that I need to do a stitched image just to get everything in the shot. In this case, I may use a wider lens for the land in order to create a smaller, more manageable stitched image.

STACKING IMAGES OF THE LAND

If you prefer not to blend exposures taken at different times of the night, you can instead capture detail in a very dark landscape by taking multiple shots and stacking them. To capture these images, you should take identical shots, one after another, of the same scene. I recommend using exposures of 1-2 minutes for each of the shots and taking at least 10 images, preferably more. The more shots you take, the more detail you'll be able to capture in the land. You can use Long Exposure Noise Reduction or a dark frame to help reduce the dark noise.

To combine the images, first select all of the photos in Lightroom, then right-click on an image and select Edit In > Open as Layers in Photoshop... When the image opens in Photoshop, select all of the layers, right click on them and select Covert to Smart Object. Then select Layer > Smart Object > Stack Modes > Median.

As long as you took all of the images with your camera firmly mounted on a tripod, you should now have a sharp image with more detail and less noise in the landscape. If the land appears blurry, the images may not all be aligned properly. In this case, you could try aligning all of them before converting to a Smart Object by selecting all of the layers and going to Edit > Auto-Align Layers... However, Photoshop may attempt to align stars that moved while you were taking the shots, making it difficult to properly align the foreground. In this case, you could first

I took this photo at Bryce Canyon National Park in Utah. I used a 24mm lens to create a stitched image of the foreground shortly after sunset. I then captured a larger stitched image of the sky using a 50mm lens a little over an hour after sunset. I carefully blended the two images in Photoshop using techniques outlined in this chapter. Canon 5D II; exposures of land: 24mm, f13, 3.2 seconds, ISO 100; exposures of sky: 50mm, f1.6, 30 seconds, ISO 6400.

delete the sky or mask out the sky from each of the layers and then try aligning the foreground.

If you want even more detailed images of the land under no moon, you can use a longer lens and stitch together multiple images that you have stacked. However, a longer lens provides less depth of field, so you won't be able to include close foreground objects in the shot (unless you do focus stacking on top of everything else). This can be a difficult and time-consuming task, but if you want to capture very detailed images of a dark landscape, it is a viable option.

When you stack images of the land, any stars in the sky will appear blurred, since they will move during the exposures. You'll therefore need to blend the land in this image with a separate image of the sky. You can blend a stacked image of the land with a single shot of the sky or with a stitched image of the sky. Or, you can blend it with a stacked image of the sky, as I'll explain next.

STACKING IMAGES OF THE SKY

You can stack images of the sky in much the same way you stack photos of the land. However, since the stars will be moving during the exposure, you'll need to use much shorter exposure times to keep the stars looking like round points of light. I recommend using the rule of 100 or 200 to calculate exposure time. This will give you very short exposures that will minimize star movement. The individual exposures will be of lower quality than those taken with the rule of 500. However, since you will be combining multiple shots, the final image will be of higher quality with almost no noticeable elongation of the stars.

Since the stars will be moving during the exposures, you'll always have to align the images in Photoshop before stacking them. If there's any foreground objects in your image, you'll need to delete or mask them out before aligning the images. Otherwise, Photoshop may try to align the foreground rather than the stars.

Even if you mask out or delete the land, Photoshop may still have trouble aligning the images. It tends to have the most trouble aligning stars in the northern or southern part of the sky, since these stars are rotating and moving at different speeds.

Another possible pitfall when using this method is that stars will move out of the frame while you are taking the shots. This can limit your total exposure time, and it can be especially problematic if you are using a longer lens which captures a smaller area of the sky.

You can get around both of these problems when stacking images by taking photos with an equatorial mount. This device is used by astrophotographers to capture stunning, detailed images of distant astronomical objects like galaxies or nebulae. However, it can also be used with a standard lens on a DSLR to capture wider images of the night sky.

An equatorial mount counteracts the earth's rotation by moving in the opposite direction and at the same rate as the rotation of the earth. This allows a lens or telescope attached to the mount to remain focused directly on an astronomical object. The objects being photographed will not become blurred or elongated, even with exposures that far exceed the rule of 500.

The simplest way to capture an image with an equatorial mount is to take one long exposure from several minutes to several hours. If the mount is properly aligned and precise enough, it will move with the motion of the stars and the photo will not be blurry. There are, however, two problems with this approach. The first is that any affordable consumer-model equatorial mount will probably not be precise enough to exactly follow the motion of the stars for a very long time. The second problem is that any long exposure over a few minutes will start to produce a lot of dark noise in the image (just as it will if you try to capture star trails with a long exposure, as explained in Chapter VII).

The solution to these problems is to take several shorter exposures of around 1-2 minutes and stack all of them onto a single image. This process is very similar to stacking images of the land. You will need to have Long Exposure Noise Reduction turned off in order to avoid a long delay after each shot. You can, however, shoot a dark frame to help reduce noise.

An equatorial mount can be especially useful if you are using a telephoto lens to photograph objects like a lunar eclipse or a comet. Without a mount, you can only do very short exposures with a telephoto lens before these objects move too much and blur.

If you use a wide angle lens with an equatorial mount, you can get significantly higher quality images than you can from a single exposure taken without one. I have found that creating large stitched images can produce photos of similar or better quality with a little less work. However, the stars will appear more elongated in a stitched image than they will in an image taken with an equatorial mount.

You can combine both of these techniques and stitch together multiple images of the sky that have been taken with an equatorial mount. This can be rather difficult, and I only recommend it for those who are very comfortable using an equatorial mount and stitching images. The effort may be worthwhile if you want to make very large prints of the photograph, as this is a way to get extremely detailed images of the night sky. If you do this, you'll need to make sure none of the stars you want to photograph will set during the time it takes to capture all of the images. So you won't want to start out photographing any stars that are near the western horizon.

Stacking Programs

You can use Photoshop to stack images taken with an equatorial mount, in the same way you stack images of the land. However, there are also many software programs designed to stack images taken with an equatorial mount. Most of these are expensive and rather difficult to use. However, there is a free program that does a good job and is easy to learn.

DeepSkyStacker

Deep Sky Stacker can be downloaded at http://deepskystacker.free.fr/. Unfortunately, it is only compatible with Windows and was not compatible Windows 8 as of this book's printing.

To use DeepSkyStacker, click on Open Picture Files... and select all of the images you want to stack. You can also add any dark frames you took by clicking on Dark Files... There are some other files you can add, including offset/bias files and flat files. Offset/bias frames can help reduce read noise in your image. You can create them by taking a shot with your lens cap and eyepiece cover on. You'll want to use the fastest shutter speed on your camera, like 1/8000 second. The other settings should be the same as the settings you use for all your other shots. With newer cameras, read noise is minimal, so I personally don't find it necessary to create these files when shooting nightscapes.

Flat frames can help reduce vignetting or uneven illumination in an image. They are somewhat difficult to create and are more important if you are using a long lens or telescope to photograph very distant objects. I don't find them necessary for nightscapes, especially since Lightroom can help eliminate vignetting. If you are interested in learning more about these files, DeepSkyStacker provides a good explanation in their help section.

Once you've loaded your images and any optional dark frames or other files, you should make sure they are all selected and click on Register Checked Pictures... I recommend using the default settings initially. I also suggest clicking on Stack After Registering, so it automatically stacks the images.

Although the default settings will usually work well, you can experiment with some of the more advanced settings once you get more familiar with this program. The help section provides an overview of the options that are available.

Equatorial Mounts

There are three popular equatorial mounts that are lightweight, affordable, and made primarily for use with DSLR cameras and lenses. I'll discuss the pros and cons of each of these.

iOptron SkyTracker

This mount is the least expensive of the three options. It has a compact, rectangular design and can currently be purchased with a polar scope for around $370. The polar scope is used to align the mount to the North Star.

The iOptron can be mounted directly onto a tripod,

so you don't need to purchase a second tripod head to use it. It is rated to hold 7.7 pounds, so it may not work as well with heavier telephoto lenses.

The build quality of the iOptron doesn't appear to be as good as the more expensive options, and the polar scope is of lower quality. That being said, it should be sufficient for most of your needs, especially if you won't be shooting with long lenses. The iOptron is probably the easiest of all the mounts to operate.

Vixen Polarie Star Tracker

This mount is similar in appearance to the iOptron but is a bit smaller and is rated to hold seven pounds. The unit appears to have a little better build quality and tracking accuracy than the iOptron. It currently sells for $389, and the polar scope costs an additional $129. Also, you will need a second tripod head to use the Vixen, so it could wind up costing quite a bit more than the iOptron. It is better if the second tripod head is a 3-way pan/tilt head, as this will make it easier to align the mount with the North Star.

Astrotrac TT320X-AG

If you want something that holds more weight, the Astrotrac may be for you. It is rated to hold 33 pounds, so it can be used with virtually any DSLR and lens combination. It also appears to have the best tracking accuracy of any of the mounts listed. This is more important when shooting with a long telephoto lens, as you don't need as much accuracy with wider lenses.

The Astrotrac is the most expensive of the three and currently sells for $580. You'll need to pay about $140 more for the polar scope. You'll also need to attach an external battery pack to the Astrotrac, as it does not have a built-in battery compartment. Like the Vixen, you'll need a second tripod head to mount the device onto your tripod.

The Astrotrac does not weigh much more than the other mounts, but it's thin and elongated, making it less portable. It also appears more delicate than the other mounts, due to its long arms.

The Astrotrac is probably most suitable for those wanting to take a large number of shots with an equatorial mount, including some with a long telephoto lens. This is the mount that I own, and it works well. However, if I were starting over I might opt for the iOptron due to its low cost and ease of use.

FOCUS STACKING

Another situation in which blending multiple exposures can be very useful is when you have a close foreground and you can't get both the foreground and background in focus in a single exposure. To get around this problem, you can take two or more shots focused at different distances and later blend the parts of each image that are in focus.

As an example, if you shoot with a 24mm lens at f1.8, the maximum depth of field you can get is from 18 feet to infinity. If you have an object closer than 18 feet in your image, you won't be able to get everything in focus. You can extend the depth of field by taking two shots, one focused at 36 feet and the other focused at 12 feet. The image focused at 36 feet will be in focus from 18 feet to infinity. The image focused at 12 feet will be in focus from 9 feet to 18 feet. You can blend these two photos to get an image that is in focus from 9 feet to infinity. In reality, you'll want to leave a lot more overlap between the areas of the image that are in focus, so as to leave room for error.

While I've calculated the exact focus distances in the example above, you don't actually have to do this. You can take the first shot focused at infinity. Then turn your focus ring to slightly less than infinity and take another shot. Keep focusing closer and closer and taking shots until you're focused at or in front of the nearest object in your image. You likely won't need to use every image you take, but by shooting this many photos you can be sure that every part of the scene will be in sharp focus in at least one of the images. You can later choose which exposures you want to use for the focus stack when you import them into the computer. You'll be able to zoom in on the photos on a large screen and see exactly how much of the shot is in focus.

If you're doing a simple focus stack with just two exposures, you should open both files in Photoshop. Select the Move tool, hold down the Shift key, and drag the image with the distant objects in focus onto the other image. The file you drag it onto will then have two layers - the top one with the distant objects in focus and the bottom one with the near objects in focus. Now, select both layers and click Edit > Auto-Align Layers... On the top layer, you'll want to mask out all of the foreground objects that are out of focus. Sometimes you can do this quickly with the brush tool. As long as you left plenty of overlap in the areas that are in focus, you don't have to be overly precise. However, you should check the image at 100% zoom to see if there are any out-of-focus areas. You can then refine the mask if necessary. If there are areas of the image that abruptly transition from near to far, you'll need to make a more precise selection using the Quick Selection Tool.

If you need to blend more than two images, you'll use the same process with more layers. On the top layer, mask out everything that is not in focus. Then repeat this on all of the layers below it.

Instead of manually blending the exposures, Photoshop has an option that lets you attempt to automatically blend them. You can select all of the layers and then click Edit > Auto-Blend Layers... Select Stack Images under Blend Method and then click OK. I have found, however, that Photoshop usually does not do a very good job focus-stacking images taken at night. There is another program you can purchase called Helicon Focus that I have heard does a better job. However, manually focus stacking images is a relatively easy task, so I have not tried this program.

ENLARGING STAR SIZE

When shooting images at night, your camera can capture far more stars than the eye can see. This is

---

I took this image with a 50mm lens at f1.8, which only allowed me to get objects from about 80 feet to infinity in focus. However, the nearest foreground object was approximately 30 feet away. I therefore had to take shots with multiple focus points and stack them. In each of the layers below, I masked out areas that were out of focus. Nikon D800e, 50mm, f1.8, 8 seconds, ISO 4000.

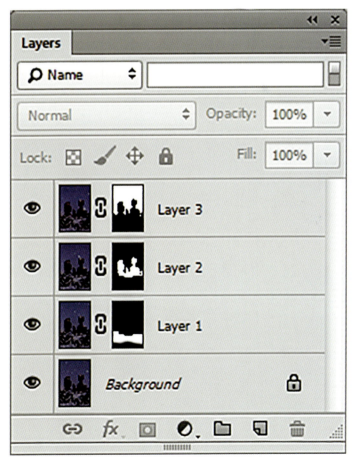

often a good thing, as it can produce really dramatic images of the Milky Way. However, this can be detrimental if you are photographing a familiar constellation or star pattern like Orion or the Big Dipper. These are easy to see with the naked eye, but they can become lost amidst all the stars that the camera can capture.

There are several ways to fix this problem. All of them involve increasing the size of the brightest stars in your image so that the constellations stand out and appear more like they do to the naked eye. A couple of these techniques involve blending multiple exposures and will be described below. There are also ways to increase star size with single exposures in post-processing. This will be described in the next chapter.

Shooting Stars Out of Focus

I've spent a lot of time in this book discussing how to get everything in sharp focus. However, it can occasionally be beneficial to shoot stars out of focus. When the stars are out of focus, they will appear larger in the image. Since there isn't much detail in the stars to begin with, you don't necessarily have to have them in perfect focus. If you take a shot with the stars out of focus, this will cause more distant objects on the land to appear out of focus as well. So you will generally have to blend two exposures - one with the land in sharp focus and one with the stars a little out of focus.

To shoot the out-of-focus stars, I recommend taking multiple exposures, while gradually shifting your focus ring from infinity to closer and closer distances. This will give you stars that are more and more out of focus, and you will have a lot more options to choose from in post-processing.

In Photoshop, you can blend the exposure for the land and the exposure for the stars, as described in the section on blending multiple shots at one time. It should actually be quite a bit easier to blend these shots than other images described in this chapter. This is because, other than the difference in focus, the two images should be quite similar to one another and easier to seamlessly combine.

If you prefer, you can only enlarge the stars that

make up the constellation or star pattern. This will allow these stars to stand out even more. To do this, in the layer with the out-of-focus stars, you'll need to mask out everything except for the stars in the constellation. I did this in the below image, but I exaggerated the effect by using stars that are larger and more out of focus than I normally would. This helped demonstrate the effect at the small size the image is printed in this book.

This image depicts the Big Dipper over Church Rock in eastern Utah. I took one shot with everything in sharp focus and a second shot with the stars out of focus. I then added only the out-of-focus stars from the Big Dipper to the shot with everything in focus. Nikon D800e, 50mm, f2.8, 10 seconds, ISO 6400.

In the image on page 80, I rendered the entire sky out of focus. This made all of the stars appear larger and helped the Big Dipper stand out a bit more (though not nearly as much is it does in the photo above).

Fog Filter

Another option for enlarging star size is to use a fog filter. As discussed in Chapter I, this filter can make bright stars appear larger and glow more. It can also make the land appear out of focus. So you'll need to take an exposure for the land without the filter and an exposure for the sky with the filter. You can then blend them as described in the previous section.

SHOOTING THE MOON

As mentioned in Chapter V, if you want to avoid overexposing the moon at night, you'll likely have to blend two exposures - one with a shutter speed of about one second for the moon and another with a longer shutter speed for the rest of the scene. This can be very difficult to accomplish, as you'll have to clone out the white blob and bright sky surrounding the moon in the second exposure. A better time to attempt this is during a lunar eclipse. During totality, an eclipse is sufficiently faint that you won't have much of a white blob and bright sky around the moon to clone out.

You could accomplish this by taking the two exposures with the same focal length lens. In Photoshop, you can place the shorter exposure on a layer above the longer exposure. Then mask out everything on the top layer except for the moon. You can also clone out some of the bright areas around the moon in the bottom layer.

While this technique seems straight forward enough, there is one problem with it. Celestial objects will usually appear larger in an image with longer exposures. This is because you don't just capture the disk of the objects but also the glow around them. In the shorter exposure of the moon, you don't capture a glow around it, so it appears smaller. In the following image, if I had simply blended two exposures with the same focal length lens, the moon would have looked barely bigger than Mars. This would look unnatural because it appears much larger than Mars to the naked eye. I therefore took the longer exposure with a 38mm lens and the shorter exposure for the moon with an 85mm lens. This made the moon appear larger in that image, and the size about matched the overexposed moon I captured with the 38mm lens. I therefore recommend taking the shorter exposure for the moon with a lens that is about twice the focal length of the lens you use for the longer exposure.

To capture this image of a total lunar eclipse, I blended an exposure of the moon with an exposure of the rest of the scene. Nikon D800e; exposure of moon: 85mm, f2.8, 1 second, ISO 500; exposure of rest of scene: 38mm, f2.8, 13 seconds, ISO 6400.

If you want the moon to appear larger, you can use an even longer lens for the shorter exposure. This can produce some dramatic images, but it can also start to make the moon appear unnaturally large.

X. Post-Processing Night Photos

There is a perception among some people today that any work done on an image in Adobe Lightroom or Photoshop will make the image "less real" and that the only "real" photos are ones that come straight out of the camera completely unaltered.

One problem with this belief is that sensors in digital cameras convert photons of light into data that is represented by a series of 0s and 1s. If you want something that is completely unaltered from what the camera recorded, it will be a series of 0s and 1s, not a photograph.

In order to produce an image, the data captured by the camera sensors must be converted into pixels, each of which contains one color value. There is no "right" way to convert the data into pixels. You can let the camera or computer software do all the work, or you can provide input into how you want the image rendered by adjusting the contrast, white balance, brightness, etc.

It is my belief that a photographer knows what it is that they were trying to capture in a photograph better than the default settings of a software program. By letting the camera or computer software render the photo, you are not producing an image that is "more real." You are instead letting software make all your artistic decisions for you. This can be especially problematic for night photos, as the software is designed to optimize photos taken during the day.

A lot of the work you do in Lightroom and Photoshop is similar to work you would do for all of your photographs. You will need to adjust the various sliders in Lightroom to begin optimizing the image. In most cases, you will then want to finalize the image in Photoshop.

There are many lengthy books devoted entirely to using Lightroom and/or Photoshop. I'm unable to cover all of this in one chapter. I will therefore focus more on post-processing techniques that are important to night photography but not often done with images taken during the day. You should then be able to combine these techniques with techniques you use to optimize all of your other photos.

Although there are other software programs available for preparing photographs, most photographers today use Lightroom and/or Photoshop. I will therefore focus on these two programs, as well as some plug-ins for these programs.

Lightroom is a software program developed by Adobe from the ground up specifically for the use of digital photographers. It is quite a bit easier to use than Photoshop, which is also intended for graphic designers and has some features that most photographers won't use. However, Photoshop is a more robust program, and you can do things with it that you cannot do in Lightroom. So I recommend owning both programs, especially for processing night photos. These photos are usually more difficult to process than daytime photos and may require more software tools.

I'll discuss the general workflow that I use to process my night photos. However, there is no "right way" to process photos. How you want your images to look is ultimately your decision. You should try to develop your own style of processing photos and create images that are most pleasing to you.

Left: The northern lights dance above the Brooks Range near Wiseman, Alaska. If I had relied on the default settings in my camera or Lightroom to process the image, it would have appeared flat and had a yellow color cast. To get the image to really stand out and convey how spectacular the northern lights are, I had to carefully process the image in Lightroom and Photoshop. Canon 5D II, 14mm, f2.8, 10 seconds, ISO 6400.

As I mentioned in the introduction, I have also created a video showing in detail how to accomplish the post-processing techniques described in this chapter and in the last three chapters. This video is available at http://www.collierpublishing.com.

LIGHTROOM ADJUSTMENTS

Many of the adjustments you do on night photos in Lightroom will be similar to adjustments you do for your daytime photos. All of the adjustment sliders I discuss can be found in Lightroom's Develop module. These sliders are identical to those found in Adobe Camera RAW, which comes with Photoshop. So if you don't own Lightroom, you can do the same adjustments with that software.

White Balance

White balance is one of the most important adjustments you will make to your night photos in Lightroom. The colors in your image may not look very good straight out of the camera, but as long as you shot in RAW, this is your chance to fix this.

If you took your image during twilight, I recommend keeping the white balance near your camera's daylight settings. This is because light from the sun will still be giving a little color to the sky. Towards the end of twilight in the evening (or the beginning of twilight in the morning) you may need to start lowering the color temperature to keep the colors looking natural.

This photograph shows the Milky Way and Venus rising above Turret Arch in Arches National Park. I used the Lightroom preset called Zeroed to show how this image looks with every slider set to zero in Lightroom, except the white balance, which was set to daylight. This photo needs quite a bit of work. The colors look a little too yellow, and I'll need to bring out a lot more contrast, especially in the Milky Way. The image also has a lot of noise. I'll be able to eliminate the noise in the foreground by making it appear as a pitch black silhouette. Canon 5D II, 14mm, f2.8, 30 seconds, ISO 6400.

If your photo was shot after twilight with the moon out, I recommend using a white balance between 4150K and 5000K. The light from the moon is just reflected sunlight, so it is comparable to daylight. However, since the moon isn't perfectly white, the reflected light has a little different temperature than sunlight. A full moon has a color temperature of about 4150K. However, I've found that using this color temperature can result in skies that appear almost neon blue. This may be how the sky would appear to us if we could see colors as well during the night as we do during the day. Since we can't, I usually use a white balance of around 4600K. This usually produces skies that seem more natural. I generally keep the tint close to my camera's daylight setting.

If you took your shot after twilight under no moon and used your camera's daylight setting, the image will usually have a yellow color cast to it. I therefore recommend lowering the temperature to reduce the yellow. If you have anything white, like snow or a waterfall, in the foreground of your image, you can hit W and click on the white area using the White Balance Selector tool. This will often give you pretty good colors in your image, but you can manually refine the white balance if necessary. If there is no obvious white area in the foreground of your image, I've found that a temperature close to 3800K will produce fairly neutral colors with limited color cast. If you reduce the temperature even more, you will start to get a bluer color to the skies. This may look more appealing, since we are used to the sky appearing blue during the day. However, the sky really doesn't have much blue in it after twilight under no moon.

If you prefer the look of blue skies after twilight under no moon, I don't recommend creating them by lowering the temperature in Lightroom. This will create a blue cast over the entire image and make the stars and Milky Way look blue. I instead recommend that you keep the temperature around 3800K. Then, in Photoshop you can add more blue to the sky using a Color Balance adjustment layer with an Expanded Darks luminosity mask. This mask will be described in more detail later in this chapter. It will prevent the adjustment from affecting bright areas of the sky, and you will be able to retain more natural colors in the stars and the Milky Way. You may also want to mask out any foreground, so it doesn't get a blue cast.

Rather than making the sky appear blue, you may be inclined to try and make it appear black, since that is how it appears to our eyes at night. However, even under no moon, the sky is not always black. If you took your photo during astronomical twilight, there will often be color in the sky left over from sunset. So you will often get red colors near the horizon and blue color in the sky. Even if you shot after twilight hours, there can be color produced by airglow. These colors are similar to the colors produced by the northern lights, but they are much fainter. They can't be seen with the naked eye, but they can be picked up by the camera.

Since we can't see any of these colors, it can be difficult to know exactly how to render them in a photograph. I recommend adjusting the sliders until you get colors that look good to you without creating an obvious color cast over the whole image. There is some artistic license involved here.

You can also adjust the tint until you get colors that look good to you. You don't want to adjust this as much as the temperature and should generally keep it near zero. I've found that a tint of +8 often works well.

Exposure

If you used the camera settings I recommended in Chapter IV, your photograph may look too bright when you first import it into Lightroom. The Exposure slider can be used to darken the image, but I don't recommend doing this just yet. In fact, as long as you're not blowing out the highlights, I recommend brightening the image even more by moving the exposure slider to the right. You can keep moving it until you have data near the right side of the histogram but are not clipping any of the highlights. This will give you better tonal range throughout the image. You'll be able to darken the photo back up, while preserving some of the tonal range, in Photoshop.

Contrast

Your images will likely look very flat when you first import them, so a big goal when processing images is to get more contrast throughout the photo. However, I don't recommend adjusting the contrast much in Lightroom, as there are more ways of doing this in Photoshop. The most I recommend increasing the contrast is to +25, but you can keep it at 0 and adjust it all later.

Highlights

The Highlights slider is a great tool if any of the highlights are blown out in the image. It can be difficult to blow out highlights at night, but it is possible, especially when shooting under a bright moon. You can tell if any highlights are clipped by looking at the histogram. If you see a small triangle on the upper right of the histogram, then you are clipping some highlights. You can click on the triangle to show exactly what highlights are blown out. You can move the Highlights slider to the left until the highlights are no longer clipped (or until you're clipping a minimal amount of highlights).

If you're forced to move the Highlights slider more than -25 to the left to avoid clipping the highlights, it indicates that you overexposed the photo in camera. In the future, you'll want to lower the ISO when shooting in similar conditions to avoid overexposing the shot.

If you are forced to adjust this slider aggressively, make sure you're not bringing out halos around high contrast edges in the image.

Shadows

The Shadows slider allows you to recover some detail in very dark shadows. This can be useful for night photos, since you will frequently have very dark areas in an image. If you see a triangle on the upper left of the histogram, then you are clipping the shadows. Again, you can click on this triangle to see what areas are clipped. You can then move the Shadows slider to the right to recover some details in the shadows.

When you bring out details in the shadows, you will also bring out more noise in the image. So be careful not to push the slider too far right. It's okay to have some very dark shadows in night photos.

If your goal is to render foreground objects as silhouettes, then you won't want any detail in the shadows. In this case, you can move the Shadows slider to the left to eliminate details and render the objects pitch black. You may also need to move the Blacks slider to the left to fully darken the foreground. When adjusting these sliders, you'll want to make sure that it doesn't cause the sky to become too dark as well. If it does, you can pull back on the sliders and leave some detail in the shadows. You can later select just the shadow areas and darken them in Photoshop.

Whites & Blacks

The Whites and Blacks sliders are similar to the Highlights and Shadows sliders, except they work on a wider range of tones in the image. I don't recommend making very significant changes to these sliders, as you will be able to fine tune things better in Photoshop.

Clarity

The Clarity slider increases localized contrast in the image, as opposed to the Contrast slider, which increases the overall contrast of the image. This slider can help make the image "pop" a little more. However, if the Clarity slider is pushed too far to the right, it can start to bring out halos in the image. So I recommend keeping this slider between 0 and +20. If you later decide you want to increase localized contrast more, I'll discuss a way to do this in Photoshop.

Vibrance & Saturation

I don't recommend adjusting the Vibrance or Saturation sliders in Lightroom. The adjustments you make in Photoshop will usually bring out the colors more. It's easier to wait until you've done those adjustments and then adjust the vibrance and saturation in Photoshop.

This is how the image from page 138 appeared after I finished working on it in Lightroom. I decreased the color temperature to 3800K to give the sky more of a neutral color. I increased the Exposure slider to +0.25 and the contrast slider to +25. I moved the Shadows slider to the left until the foreground appeared as a black silhouette. I also clicked on Enable Profile Corrections in the Lens Correction panel. This helped remove some of the vignetting in the corners.

Sharpening

You can apply some sharpening to your photos in Lightroom. Since you will do final sharpening later, you don't want to sharpen your images too much at this point.

The sharpening sliders are located under the Detail panel in Lightroom's Develop module. I generally use these settings for all of my night photos:

Amount: 25
Radius: 1.0
Detail: 25
Masking: 0

Noise Reduction

Lightroom has some noise reduction features that can be useful for night photos, especially if you don't own other noise reduction software. There are two noise reduction sliders called Luminance and Color. The Luminance slider attempts to reduce unnatural fluctuations in the brightness of the image. This noise is often the result of photon noise, which occurs when shooting in low light. The Color slider attempts to reduce chrominance noise, which can appear as hot pixels or unnatural color variations. This noise can be the result of dark noise that is produced during very long exposures.

The Luminance slider can be effective at reducing noise, but it can also blur some of the details in the image. I have found that Topaz DeNoise does a better job at reducing this noise without blurring details. So I recommend keeping this slider set at zero. If you choose not to purchase Topaz DeNoise, you can adjust this slider. Make sure you don't blur any details too much, especially in the foreground. If you're blurring details in the foreground, you may instead want to use the Noise slider that is available with the Adjustment Brush. This will allow you to do more noise reduction on the sky, where you don't have to worry as much about blurring details.

The Color slider doesn't blur details too much, so you can use this slider in Lightroom, even if you're also using Topaz DeNoise. I usually keep the Color sliders at their default settings, which are:

Color: 25
Detail: 50
Smoothness: 50

This will usually be effective at reducing small amounts of chrominance noise in your image. If your photo has a lot of chrominance noise, you can increase the amount of noise reduction. However, this can cause some unwanted fringing along edges in the image. So make sure the noise reduction isn't adversely affecting parts of the photo, especially in the stars and along areas where it transitions from land to sky.

Lens Corrections

The Lens Corrections panel in the Develop module of Lightroom can be very useful for night photos. Even with the best lenses, night photos often have strong vignetting in the corners and sometimes have chromatic aberration. Some of the wide angle lenses that you use in night photography can also cause noticeable distortion in the images.

The easiest way to fix vignetting and distortion is to click on Profile in the Lens Correction panel and then check the box that says Enable Profile Corrections. This will attempt to fix any vignetting and distortion based on properties of the lens that you used. If the vignetting and distortion is not properly fixed, you can fine tune the image by adjusting the Distortion and Vignetting sliders at the bottom of the panel.

If Lightroom does not automatically bring up the lens that you used for the shot, you will have to manually enter the lens under Make and Model. If Lightroom does not have your lens in its database, you will need to manually adjust the vignetting by clicking on Manual and then adjusting the Lens Vignetting sliders. You can also adjust the Transform sliders if you want to try and correct any distortion from the lens. This is useful if you have straight lines, like trees or the horizon, in your image that you want to remain straight.

The Lens Corrections panel can also be used to fix chromatic aberration in an image. In night photos, chromatic aberration will usually appear as an unnatural magenta color around the edges of stars. To fix this, click on Color in the Lens Correction panel. You will see a box you can click that says Remove Chromatic Aberration. This will usually do a good job of fixing any problems in an image taken during the day. However, it doesn't tend to work very well for chromatic aberration around stars. You'll usually have more success if you adjust the Defringe sliders. Oftentimes, simply changing the Amount sliders under Defringe will do a good job fixing unnatural colors around stars. You should adjust the sliders the minimum amount required to remove this color. If this doesn't work, you can also adjust the Purple Hue and Green Hue sliders until you get a result you like.

Lightroom Presets

When processing night photos, you'll likely find that you are using similar settings for a lot of images. You can save these settings as a Lightroom preset, so that you can start off with these settings. You can do this by selecting a photo that has the settings you want to use for the preset. Then locate the Presets panel in the upper left corner of the Develop module. Click '+' on the upper right of this panel. In the box that opens, you'll need to give a name to the preset and then select all of the settings that you want applied to the preset. Now click Create, and this preset will show up in the User Presets collection in the Presets panel. You can now apply this preset to any other photos by selecting the photos and clicking on the preset. You can apply multiple presets to the same image if they affect different settings in Lightroom.

You can also apply a preset when importing photos. To do this, click Ctrl+Shift+I (Cmd+Shift+I on a Mac) to import photos. Then, select the preset in the drop-down box next to Develop Settings in the Apply During Import panel.

You might start by creating your own preset for photos taken with and without a moon in the sky.

David Kingham offers some donationware presets for night photography. You can find these presets at http://www.davidkinghamphotography.com/night-photography-lightroom-presets/. Most of these presets are designed to make the image look as good as possible in Lightroom. The settings I've recommended are only designed to prepare the image for further editing in Photoshop. So if you plan to work on the image in Photoshop, I recommend starting with the settings that I've outlined previously in this chapter.

If you don't own Photoshop or prefer to do most of the work in Lightroom, David Kingham's presets can be very useful. However, I recommend that you start off without using presets. By doing all of the adjustments yourself, you can get a better feel for how altering each slider can affect the image. You can also start to develop your own personal style for processing images.

Other Lightroom Features

There are a lot of other features in the Develop module of Lightroom, including the ability to do localized adjustments with the Adjustment Brush. However, you have greater control over localized adjustments in Photoshop. If you don't own Photoshop or aren't yet comfortable with it, the Adjustment Brush can be useful to work on selective parts of your image.

PHOTOSHOP ADJUSTMENTS

Once you've finished making preliminary adjustments in Lightroom, you can begin working on your image in Photoshop. To open an image in Photoshop, right-click on the image in Lightroom and select Edit In > Edit in Adobe Photoshop...

In addition to adjustments in Photoshop, I'll also discuss adjustments you can make using Photoshop plug-ins made by third-party companies. Once installed, these plug-ins can be used within Photoshop.

Noise Reduction

After opening an image in Photoshop, I first try to reduce the noise as much as possible without blurring the details. To do this, I recommend using a plug-in known as Topaz DeNoise. This software can be purchased at http://www.topazlabs.com/denoise/. If you don't own Photoshop, Topaz DeNoise can also be used as a Lightroom plug-in.

I've tested other noise reduction software, and many of these programs blur a lot of the details in the image in addition to reducing the noise. However, Topaz DeNoise does a remarkable job of keeping the details intact while also significantly reducing noise.

Once you've installed Topaz DeNoise, you will be able to access it in the Filter menu of Photoshop under Topaz Labs > Topaz DeNoise.

When a photo is opened in Topaz DeNoise, you will see a list of presets on the left side of the screen. You can try the various RAW presets and see which one works best. There will be a preview of how your image will appear in the center of the screen. If you click on this image, it will show the original, unaltered image, and when you let go of the mouse button it will go back to the preview with noise reduction applied.

I recommend using the strongest RAW preset that

doesn't noticeably blur the details in the photo. Usually, one of the presets will work for your image, but you can fine-tune the noise reduction using the sliders on the right side of the screen.

Once the preview looks good, simply click OK, and it will process your image and return you to Photoshop.

Levels Adjustment with Luminosity Masks

Now that you have minimized the noise, you can start optimizing the appearance of the image using adjustment layers. The first adjustment layer I usually create is a Levels layer. To create an adjustment layer, go to Layer > New Adjustment Layer and select the layer you want to create. Alternatively, you can click on the circular black and white icon at the bottom of the Layers panel and select your adjustment layer from there.

Once you've opened a Levels layer, you will see a histogram of your image in the Properties panel (this was called the Adjustments panel in Photoshop CS4 and CS5). The histogram for many night photos, especially those shot under no moon or a faint moon, will have a lot of data on the far left side (representing darker pixels in your image) and a very small amount of data extending to the right side of the histogram (representing lighter pixels like those from stars, planets, or meteors). A histogram like this generally means that you have a flat, low contrast image. Images that are more appealing to people usually have more data extending towards the right side of the histogram. These photos will have more contrast and stronger midtones.

A simple way to spread more of the data to the right side of the histogram is to move the right slider in the Levels palette to the left. However, this will clip the highlights in the image and cause them to be blown out. You need to be able to mask out the brightest parts of the image so that they will not be affected by the Levels adjustment and therefore not get blown out. You can do this using

---

After optimizing the Turret Arch photo in Lightroom, I began working on it in Photoshop. I first used Topaz DeNoise to reduce the noise in the sky. My next goal was to bring out more contrast in the image and make the Milky Way more prominent. To accomplish this, I created a Levels adjustment using the Expanded Darks luminosity mask, as seen in the panels on the left.

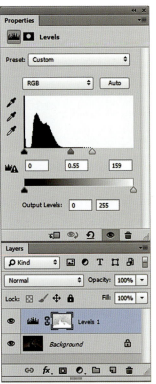

something popularized by Tony Kuyper known as a luminosity mask.

You can find Tony's tutorial on luminosity masks, as well as Photoshop actions you can use to create them at http://goodlight.us/writing/luminositymasks/luminositymasks-1.html.

For the Levels adjustments, I usually start by using the Expanded Darks luminosity mask. If you've installed Tony's Photoshop actions, you can create this mask by going to the Actions palette in Photoshop and selecting Expanded Darks under TK-LumMasks(Layers). Then, click on the Play button, and the mask will be created in a new Curves layer. You will need to move the mask to the Levels layer by clicking on the mask in the Curves layer and dragging it to the Levels layer.

Now, you can simply drag the right slider to the left in the Levels panel, as described previously. You'll probably also need to drag the center slider a good distance to the right in order to make the image look darker. You can adjust the sliders back and forth until you get an image that you are pleased with. Make sure not to slide the right slider so far left that it is clipping data that is seen on the histogram. The farthest you'll generally want to slide it is near the rightmost edge of the part of the histogram that contains data, as seen in the sample Levels adjustment on the previous page. However, sometimes you won't want to drag it this far, as it can make parts of the image appear too bright for a night shot.

Oftentimes, a single Levels adjustment with the Expanded Darks luminosity mask will significantly improve the image, and this will be the only Levels layer you need to use. However, sometimes the photo will still look too flat. In this case, you might instead try using a Darks mask or Dark Darks mask.

If the image still appears flat, you might try creating two Levels layers with two different masks. The first mask could be an Expanded Darks mask, and the second could be a Dark Darks mask, as seen in the example on the following page.

I should point out that creating multiple Levels layers like this can potentially start to degrade image quality and produce banding or an image that looks overworked. It is better if you can make the adjustments you need with a single Levels layer. However, night photos can be tricky to process, and sometimes adding a second or even third Levels layer with different luminosity masks can be worthwhile.

Curves

After you make the Levels adjustment, you should have an image that has a lot more contrast. If it still doesn't have quite as much contrast as you like, you can do a Curves adjustment. To increase mid-tone contrast, you can create what is known as an S-Curve. Click on a point on the lower left of the diagonal line in the Curves box. For night photos, you'll generally want his point to be far down and close to the bottom left of the box. Now, drag this point down.

Next, click on a point on the upper right of the diagonal line and drag this point up. For night photos, I generally recommend clicking on a point about 3/4 of the way up this line. You can then adjust these two points in the Curves box and see how it changes the photo. Keep adjusting them until the image looks good to you.

There are also some presets you can use in the Curves panel in the drop-down box next to Curves. The Increase Contrast (RGB) preset is similar to the one I just described. I recommend using the presets only as a starting point and adjusting the curve as necessary to optimize the image you're working on.

Vibrance

After you do Levels and/or Curves adjustments, you'll likely notice that the colors "pop" and appear more saturated. If you want to further adjust the saturation, you can use the Vibrance adjustment layer.

This layer has two sliders called Vibrance and Saturation. The Saturation slider increases the saturation of all colors in the image the same amount. The Vibrance slider, on the other hand, increases less saturated parts of the image more than parts that already have a lot of saturation. This helps prevent any one color from becoming oversaturated and having a "Disney" look to it. I recommend adjusting this slider first. If you can't get the look you want, you can also adjust the Saturation slider until things look right.

Dodging & Burning

Dodging and burning refers to a technique film photographers used when they printed their photographs in a darkroom. They would dodge parts of the image to make it lighter and burn other parts to make it darker. This technique can be easily mimicked in Photoshop.

If you installed Tony Kuyper's luminosity masks, it should also come with a Burn/Dodge action that will create a Burn/Dodge layer. If you don't have this action, it is very easy to make the layer manually. Simply create a blank layer by hitting Ctrl+Shift+N (Cmd+Shift+N on a Mac). Then change the blending mode of the layer to Soft Light.

Once you've created this layer, you can paint on it with a white paintbrush to lighten parts of the image. You can use a black paintbrush to darken parts of the image. I recommend setting the Opacity of the paintbrush to 5% and the Hardness to 0%. If the Opacity is too high, the effect can be too extreme. If the Hardness is set too high, it can produce obvious edges along areas where you did the dodging and burning.

The manner in which you use a Burn / Dodge layer is largely an artistic decision. Carefully inspect your image and decide if there are parts that could benefit from darkening or lightening. Sometimes, parts of the sky will appear too light and could benefit from some burning. Alternatively, parts of the foreground may appear too dark, and you may choose to dodge them. Be careful, though, as dodging can bring out more noise in the image.

Although the Levels adjustment I did on the previous page helped the image quite a bit, I still felt that it looked too flat. I therefore did a second Levels adjustment, this time using the Dark Darks luminosity mask.

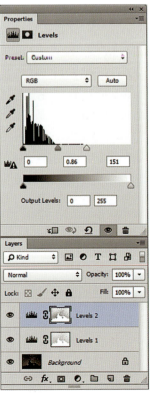

If there is still some vignetting in the corners of the image that you were unable to remove in Lightroom, you can dodge those areas to lighten them. Some photographers, on the other hand, like a little vignetting in the image and will intentionally choose to burn the corners.

Dodging and burning can be particularly useful with stitched images. Sometimes, the luminosity of the sky will appear uneven after you stitch an image. By carefully dodging and burning the sky, you can get it to appear more even and natural looking.

Dodging and burning can also be useful with light paintings. The lighting may appear uneven over the scene. You can even out the lighting and make it less obvious that it was lit by artificial light.

Boosting Star Size & Brightness

If the stars don't appear large enough or bright enough to you in the image, there are some relatively easy ways to boost their size and brightness. This can be useful for bringing out more stars in the image or for selectively increasing the brightness of stars in a constellation or star pattern.

Select Stars with Light Luminosity Masks

One way to boost the size of the stars in an image is to use the luminosity masks described previously in this chapter. You'll need to create a Curves layer with a Bright Lights or Super Lights luminosity mask. This will mask out everything but the very brightest parts of your image. Since stars will often be the only really bright parts of your image, this is a quick way to select the stars. The Bright Lights Mask will select more stars than the Super Lights Mask, but it could potentially select bright parts of the image that are not stars.

Now you can right-click on the mask and select Add Mask to Selection. Then, on the Photoshop menu go to Select > Modify > Expand. Next to Expand By enter 1 pixels and hit OK. Now, go to Select > Modify > Feather, and again enter 1 pixels and hit OK.

You can experiment with slightly larger values for expanding and feathering the selection. If you expand it more, the stars will appear larger, and if you feather it more, the glow around the stars will increase. Generally, values of 1 or 2 will be the largest you want to enter. Larger values can make the stars appear unnatural.

Once you're happy with the selection, you should set the foreground color to white. You can do this by clicking on the very small black and white squares located above the larger black and white squares on the Tools panel. If necessary, click once on the arrows next to the small black and white squares to change the large top square to white. Now, hit Alt+Backspace (Opt+Delete on a Mac). This will expand and feather the mask around the stars.

Now, bring up the Properties panel by double-clicking on the Curves icon on the Curves layer. You should click on a point in the middle of the line in the Curves box and drag it up and to the left. This will brighten the stars in the image. Avoid dragging the curve up so high that it forms a straight line at the very top. This could cause you to blow out the highlights and lose some color in the stars. If you end up brightening areas of the image that you don't want brightened, you can mask this out by painting on the mask with a black paintbrush.

If the stars still aren't bright enough, you can duplicate the Curves layer one or more times by selecting it and hitting Ctrl+J (Cmd+J on a Mac).

Selecting the stars with luminosity masks may not have any effect on the faintest stars in your image, as they may not get selected.

Select Stars with Color Range

Another way to brighten stars is to click on the Background layer and then select the stars by going to Select > Color Range... A dialog box will open and the Eyedropper tool will appear when you hover the mouse over the image. Hit Ctrl++ (Cmd++ on a Mac) to zoom in on the image. Now, click on one of the stars to select every star that has a similar color to that one. There will likely be

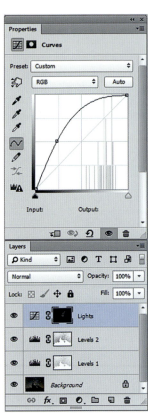

Although the Levels adjustments with luminosity masks made the Milky Way more visible, I decided I wanted to make it even more prominent. I therefore used a Bright Lights mask to select only the bright parts of the image. I then painted over everything but the Milky Way on this mask with a black paintbrush, so as to mask out everything but the bright parts of the Milky Way. I then dragged the line in the Curves panel up to brighten the brightest parts of the Milky Way. This allowed it to really stand out from the dark sky surrounding it. This is not an adjustment I make frequently, but I decided it could help this image since I had photographed a dimmer part of the Milky Way.

---

stars with different colors in your image. So you can hold down the Shift key and click on stars with different colors to select all stars with these colors.

You can select more stars by increasing the value on the Fuzziness slider or fewer stars by decreasing this value. Also, you can view all of the stars that you have selected by changing the Selection Preview at the bottom of the dialog box to Black Matte. Make sure you are not selecting more than just the stars. If you are, you can try selecting fewer colors or decreasing the Fuzziness slider. Sometimes, other colors in the image will be too close to the colors of the stars, and it will be difficult not to select them as well. In this case, you can later mask these areas out.

Once you're satisfied with your selection, hit OK. You will once again want to expand and feather the selection by 1 or 2 pixels, as described in the previous section.

Now you can create a Curves layer. It will automatically mask out everything but what you have selected. To brighten the stars, once again click on a point in the middle of the line in the Curves box and drag it up and to the left. You can duplicate this layer if needed to brighten the stars more.

I have found that selecting the stars using color range can be a little more difficult than selecting stars using luminosity masks. However, it can be preferable in some circumstances. Selecting stars with color range can give you a little more control over what stars you select. You have the option to select only stars of a certain color. Also, you can usually select fainter stars than you can with luminosity masks. This could be good if you shot under a full moon or during twilight and didn't capture as many stars as you'd like. Increasing the brightness of the faintest stars can make it appear like there are more stars in the sky.

One problem with using Color Range to select stars is that if only part of a star gets selected, it can appear blotchy when you increase the brightness. So be careful not to overdo the adjustments, and always check the images at 100% zoom to make sure you didn't introduce any unnatural artifacts into the image. If there are too many problems, you may be better off selecting the stars using luminosity masks. This may not bring out the faintest stars, but it can still bring out quite a few more stars in the image.

Selecting Individual Stars

If you only want to increase the brightness of the stars that make up constellations or star patterns, this can be achieved without much difficulty. You can select the individual stars in the constellation using the Quick Select tool. Then once again, expand and feather the selection by 1 or 2 pixels and create a Curves layer. Drag the line in the Curves box up and duplicate the layer if necessary.

Star Spikes Pro

Another option for enlarging star size is a Photoshop plug-in for PCs called Star Spikes Pro. This program allows you to create spikes around the stars similar to a sunstar effect. If you select a large number of spikes and make the length of the spikes short, it can enlarge the star size without creating noticeable spikes. This program has a lot of other features you can experiment with that can be useful for night photos.

Minimizing Light Pollution

If you're unable to get far away from city lights, you'll likely have light pollution in your images. Light pollution generally appears as a yellow, orange, or red hue in the sky.

If you have a large amount of light pollution in an image, it can be nearly impossible to eliminate in post-processing. But if you only have a small amount, it can be reduced or eliminated without too much difficulty.

The easiest way I've found to eliminate small amounts of light pollution is to create a new layer in Photoshop by hitting Ctrl+Shift+N (Cmd+Shift+N on a Mac). Now, change the layer's blending mode to Color. With this blending mode, the changes you make will only affect the color of the image and nothing else. Now, you can select the Brush tool and set the Hardness to 0% and the Opacity to around 30%. Then, Alt-click (Opt-click on a Mac) on a part of the sky where the color looks good in order to set this color as your foreground color. On the new layer, you can paint over the area where the light pollution is to make the color of that part of the sky closer to the color you set as your foreground color. You can then alt-click on another part of the sky where the color looks good and repeat as necessary until you have minimized the light pollution.

The area of the sky with light pollution may still look brighter than the rest of the sky. If it does, you can use the Burn/Dodge Layer to darken it up.

Although this is my preferred method for eliminating light pollution, there are other ways to accomplish this. If you prefer to keep some of the color from the light pollution, but don't want it to stand out as much, you can use a Hue/Saturation Layer to selectively desaturate the areas with light pollution. Depending on the color of the light pollution, you can desaturate just the reds, yellows, or magentas. You can do this by selecting the color you want to work on in the drop-down menu where it says Master. You can also drag the sliders at the bottom of the panel to select a different color range. If you find that the adjustment adversely affected other parts of the image, you can create a layer mask to mask out those areas.

Minimizing Chrominance Noise

The methods for eliminating light pollution can

also be effective at minimizing chrominance noise in a photograph. Chrominance noise will often result from dark noise in longer exposures and can appear as an unnatural red or magenta color over parts of the image. You can attempt to minimize this unnatural color using a new layer with the blending mode set to Color, in the same way you would do for light pollution.

Chrominance noise can also appear as hot pixels, where just one or a few pixels take on a much more vibrant color than neighboring pixels. Noise reduction software usually does a good job of eliminating or minimizing a small number of hot pixels. If it doesn't, you can simply clone out the hot pixels using the Clone Stamp or Healing Brush tool.

If you took a really long exposure, there could be so many hot pixels that they are almost impossible to eliminate with noise reduction software or cloning. In this case, you would need to have taken a dark frame or used Long Exposure Noise Reduction to be able to further minimize the hot pixels. If you didn't do this, you can attempt to take a dark frame later. Try to shoot in similar temperatures as you did when you shot the original image and use the exact same camera settings as you did for the original shot. More information on taking dark frames was provided on page 59.

Minimizing Luminance Noise

Luminance noise will appear as an unnatural brightness variation, or blotchiness, in a photo. The best way to minimize luminance noise is usually with noise reduction software like Topaz DeNoise. However, there is a way to more aggressively reduce this noise if you have an area of an image with minimal detail that has a very smooth and even tone. This could be the case if you have a large field of snow in your image or if you have nondescript clouds that are fairly uniform in brightness. In these areas, any luminance noise will appear more pronounced, since your eye doesn't expect to see much variation in brightness over such smooth areas.

The method for reducing luminance noise in Photoshop is very similar to the method for minimizing chrominance noise or light pollution. For this explanation, I'll assume you're reducing noise in a field of snow. Make a new, blank layer, but change the blending mode to Luminosity instead of Color. Now, select the Brush tool and set the Hardness to 0% and the Opacity to around 20%. Then, alt-click on a part of the snow that has the brightness you want. Paint over the rest of the snow field with the brush, and it will even out the luminosity of the snow. Paint over it a second or third time with the same brush color selected if you want to smooth it out even more.

You should avoid using this technique in any areas of the image where there is detail that you want to preserve. It can significantly blur the detail and is therefore only effective in limited situations.

Minimizing Star Trails

Even if you used the rule of 500 to try and render the stars as round points of light, you will see that the stars are still elongated when you zoom in on them. There is a remarkably easy way to shorten these star trails and make the stars look like round points of light. However, this technique can degrade the image quality, so it should be used only if the star trails are a noticeable problem.

First, open the image in Photoshop and create a duplicate layer by right-clicking on the Background Layer and selecting Duplicate Layer... Change the blending mode of this layer to Darken. Then, select the Move tool and use the arrow keys on your keyboard to move the layer in the direction of the star trails. As you move the layer, you will see the star trails start to reduce in size. Keep moving the layer until the stars appear as round points of light. That's it!

If you have foreground objects that are not dark silhouettes, you'll have to mask them out on the new layer. Otherwise, the foreground will appear blurred and out of focus.

You may also have problems with this technique if you used a wide angle lens or the camera was

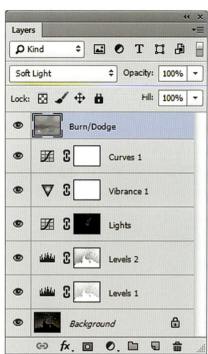

Once I had the Milky Way looking like I wanted, I focused on finalizing the image. The adjustments I had done to this point had made the bottom part of the sky look much brighter than the top. I therefore used a Burn/Dodge layer to even out the brightness. I also boosted the Vibrance and Saturation a little and used a Curves layer to increase the overall contrast a bit more.

---

pointing north or south. In this case, star trails in different parts of the sky may be moving in different directions and may be of different lengths. In this case, you'll have to do this adjustment over several smaller parts of the image. You'll want to mask out each adjustment so that it is only affecting star trails that are pointing in the same direction and are of about the same length. This can make the process a lot more difficult.

One final issue you may encounter with this method is that you may see duplicate stars at the edges of the image. Since the problem area will only be a few pixels wide, you can easily crop it out.

Converting to Black & White

Although I don't discuss black and white images much in this book, you can get some very dramatic black and white photos at night. Since our ability to see color at night is very limited, black and white photos can actually appear closer to what we see with the naked eye.

You can convert a photo to black and white in either Lightroom or Photoshop. You can do this in Lightroom by clicking on B&W in the HSL / Color / B&W panel. Lightroom will automatically try to convert it to a pleasing black and white photograph, and it often does a good job. However, you'll usually want to fine-tune the image by adjusting the color sliders. The color sliders let you decide how bright you want different color tones in your image to look when converted to black and white. For example, if you want areas in the image that are red to appear brighter in the black and white image, you can move the Red slider to the right. Alternatively, if you want these color tones to appear darker, just move the slider to the left.

If you convert an image to black and white in Lightroom and then open it in Photoshop, you cannot recover the colors or adjust the conversion settings later. You'll have to go back to the original version in Lightroom. It may therefore be easier to convert to black and white in Photoshop. You can do this using the Black & White adjustment layer, which converts the image to black and white in a similar way to Lightroom. It doesn't automatically try and produce the most pleasing result in Photoshop. However, it will attempt to do this if you click Auto in the Adjustments panel. Again, you'll likely want to fine-tune the results.

I took this shot of a remote rock formation near Moab, Utah on a spring night. I used a flashlight to illuminate the rock and focus stacked four images to increase the depth of field. I decided to convert it to black and white to keep the focus on the patterns and textures. Nikon D800e, 15mm, f2.8, 13 seconds, ISO 6400.

Since Lightroom and Photoshop convert images to black and white a little differently, you may want to try converting the image in both programs and see which one you like best. There's also a plug-in that works with Photoshop or Lightroom called Nik Silver Efex Pro that will give you a lot more options when converting to black and white. This software costs $149 and comes bundled with six other Nik plug-ins. You can get a trial of this program at https://www.google.com/nikcollection/.

Sharpening

The final global adjustment you should make to any image is to sharpen it. You will need to sharpen the image differently depending on how you plan to use it. Learning how to properly sharpen images for different outputs can be difficult. I therefore recommend Photoshop plug-ins like PhotoKit Sharpener or Nik Sharpener Pro, which can do advanced sharpening routines for you.

PhotoKit Sharpener

PhotoKit Sharpener 2 can be purchased for $99 at http://pixelgenius.com/sharpener2/. After you install it, you can access it in Photoshop by going to File > Automate > PhotoKit Output Sharpener 2... You will see a drop down menu next to Set that gives you four main sharpening options - Contone, Inkjet, Halftone, and Web and Multimedia.

You will want to use Contone for most photographic prints that are not made by inkjet printers. Inkjet should be used whenever making inkjet prints. You'll need to use Halftone for most commercial printing presses, like those that produce books or magazines. Web and Multimedia should be used if you won't be printing the photo but will display it on the computer or with a projector.

Sharpening can make the noise in an image more noticeable. If there are areas of your image where noise is prominent when viewing the photo at 50% zoom, you can partially mask out some of the sharpening. It is preferable to mask out areas that don't have much detail, such as the sky or snow. Masking out areas that have a lot of detail can make the image appear soft, so I avoid doing this.

In addition to the Output Sharpener, PhotoKit has two other sharpening options called Capture Sharpener and Creative Sharpener. Capture Sharpener works well for pre-sharpening your image when you first open it in Photoshop. You don't need to use this if you've already applied some sharpening in Lightroom. The Creative Sharpener can be used to achieve specific effects on parts or all of the image. It can be used to add a little more sharpening to the corners of the image, which will often appear softer in night photos. It could also be used to draw more attention to one part of the photo. However, since sharpening can bring out more noise, I don't often use Creative Sharpener on night photos. I find it more useful on daytime photos.

Nik Sharpener Pro

Nik Sharpener works in a similar fashion to PhotoKit Sharpener. You can sharpen the image for different output devices, and it has some creative sharpening options. I usually prefer the look of images sharpened with PhotoKit Sharpener. I think Nik Sharpener can oversharpen the image at the default settings. This can be problematic for night photos, as it can bring out more noise. To avoid this, I recommend setting the Viewing Distance to Up to 60 cm, regardless of the actual viewing distance. You may also need to reduce the Overall Sharpening Strength.

Nik Sharpener may be a better value, as it comes bundled with six other Nik plug-ins, including Silver Efex Pro. You can get the trial version or purchase this software at: https://www.google.com/nikcollection/.

Unsharp Mask

After I use PhotoKit Sharpener or Nik Sharpener, I often do one final sharpening using the Unsharp Mask filter in Photoshop. This filter can be accessed by going to Filter > Sharpen > Unsharp Mask. The settings I normally use are:

Amount: 5%-30%
Radius: 40-100 pixels
Threshold: 0 levels

The higher you set the amount, the stronger the effect will be. By using a large radius of 40 or more pixels, you will not be sharpening the fine details

in the photo. This was already done in PhotoKit Sharpener or Nik Sharpener. Rather, you will increase the localized contrast in the image and make it "pop." This is similar to what the Clarity slider does in Lightroom, but I think this method produces more pleasing effects. It can, however, create halos along high contrast edges between the foreground and sky, which you should mask out. It can also cause some highlights to appear too bright or become blown out. If this occurs, you can apply an Expanded Darks luminosity mask so it doesn't affect the bright areas of the image.

Smart Sharpen

If you don't use PhotoKit Sharpener or Nik Sharpener, the Smart Sharpen filter in Photoshop can be useful for sharpening night photos. It has a Reduce Noise slider that attempts to minimize any extra noise that is brought out during sharpening. You should avoid overdoing this, or it can blur the details. You should keep the Radius at around 1 pixel to sharpen the fine details. Determining the exact settings does require some expertise, though. The printing process can make the image appear less sharp, so you'll often need to compensate by oversharpening the photo.

Sharpening in Lightroom

If you prefer, you can do final sharpening in Lightroom. This is an easier option than Photoshop if you don't own PhotoKit Sharpener or Nik Sharpener. In the Export dialog box and in the Print and Web modules, you have the option to select Low, Standard, or High sharpening. Standard sharpening works well for most projects, though you might use High if you'll be doing any halftone printing.

Final Review

Once you've finished sharpening you should do a final review of your image. Zoom in to 100%, and view every part of the image. Check for any dust spots on the photo or any other issues with the image. Sharpening can bring out imperfections in the image. However, these can usually be easily corrected with a healing brush.

Appendix

RESOURCES

I've provided below a list of all of the apps, websites, software programs, and photography equipment that I discussed in the book. You can also find this list with clickable links at the below URL. This site will be continually updated with new products that I recommend.

http://www.gcollier.com/gear/

VIDEO TUTORIALS

I've produced a video tutorial that gives step-by-step instructions for the post-processing techniques described in this book and a few new ones. It can be bought at:

http://www.collierpublishing.com/

STARRY NIGHTS CALENDAR

I produce the Starry Nights Wall Calendar, which contains dates of all the major celestial events that you may want to photograph. This can also be found at:

http://www.collierpublishing.com/

WORKSHOPS

The Colorado Photography Festival takes place each year in mid-August, and it always offers one or more workshops on night photography. Find out more at:

http://www.coloradophotographyfestival.com

CAMERA EQUIPMENT

Cameras

Digital
Canon 1Dx, 5D Mark III, 6D
Nikon D3s, D4s, D610, D750, D800, D800e, D810, Df
Sony A7R, A7S

Film
Canon EOS 620, 630, 650
Nikon F100, FM, FM10, or N80/F80,

Lenses

Canon
EF 50mm f/1.8 II

Nikon
Nikkor 14-24mm f2.8, Nikkor 20mm f/1.8G
Nikkor 50mm f/1.8D, Nikkor 58mm f/1.4G

Rokinon/Samyang/Bower
12mm f/2.8 Fisheye, 14mm f/2.8
24mm f/1.4, 35mm f/1.4
50mm f/1.4, 85mm f/1.4

Sigma
8mm f/3.5 Circular Fisheye
20mm f/1.8, 35mm f/1.4

Tamron
150-600mm f/5.0-6.3

Tokina
11-20mm f/2.8 DX (for cropped sensors)

Tripod Legs

Feisol carbon fiber
Gitzo carbon fiber

Ball Heads

Acratech Ultimate Ballhead
Manfrotto 498RC2

Accessories

Astrotrac TT320X-AG
GigaPan EPIC Pro Robotic Camera Mount
iOptron SkyTracker
Kenko Pro Softon Type-A filter
Neewer Digital Timer Remote
Neewer Remote Control 433MHz Wire/Wireless
Neewer Shutter Release Remote Control
Novoflex EOS/NIK-NT Lens Adapter
Tiffen Double Fog 3 filter
Tiffen Grid Star Effect filter

Vixen Polarie Star Tracker
Zeikos battery grip

LIGHTING EQUIPMENT

Britek PS-200B Battery Powered Strobe Light
Coast HL7 Focusing 196 Lumen LED Headlamp
EagleTac D25C Clicky Neutral White
EagleTac G25C2 MKII Neutral White
LED Lenser P7 LED Flashlight
Luminar Work 69286 Rechargeable Spotlight
Neewer 160 LED Panel
Nitecore Tiny Monster TM26
Proton Pro (for preserving night vision)
Roscolux Swatchbook
Rosco Cinegel Swatchbook (Large) 3x5"
Vizeri VZ230

CLOTHING

Heat Factory Pop-Top Mittens with Glove Liner
NEOS Overshoes
Verseo ThermoGloves

SURVIVAL GEAR

Fast Find Personal Locator Beacon
SPOT Satellite GPS Messenger

WEBSITES

astroclub.tau.ac.il/ephem/LunarOcc/PlanetsConj/
auroraforecast.gi.alaska.edu/
blue-marble.de/nightlights/ (light pollution)
ClearDarkSky.com (cloud forecast)
djlorenz.github.io/astronomy/lp2006/ (light pollution)
dofmaster.com/dofjs.html (depth of field calculator)
DxOMark.com (equipment reviews)
go-astronomy.com/solar-system/planets-conjunctions.htm
heavens-above.com (satellites)
SeaSky.org/astronomy/astronomy-calendar-current.html
stardate.org/nightsky/meteors/
swpc.noaa.gov/products/30-minute-aurora-forecast
tidesonline.noaa.gov/
timeanddate.com/eclipse/list.html
VolcanoDiscovery.com
WeatherUnderground.com

SOFTWARE PROGRAMS

Auto Pano Pro
Deep Sky Stacker
Google Earth
Helicon Focus
Hugin
Lightroom
Magic Lantern
Microsoft Image Composite Editor (ICE)
Photoshop
PT Gui
StarStaX
Startrails.exe
Stellarium
The Photographer's Ephemeris

PHOTOSHOP PLUG-INS

Advanced Stacker Plus
Astronomy Tools Actions Set
Floris Van Breugel's Star Trail Stacker
Nik Sharpener Pro
Nik Silver Efex Pro
PhotoKit Sharpener 2
Sam Waguila's StarTrail Stacker
Star Spikes Pro
Tony Kuyper's Luminosity Masks
Topaz DeNoise

ITUNES APPS

3D Sun
Aurora Forecast
Dark Sky Finder
Google Earth
myCSC
PhotoPills
Stellarium
Triggertrap
Weather Underground

ANDROID APPS

Aurora Alert
Aurora Buddy
Clear Sky Droid
DSLR Remote
Google Earth
Loss of the Night
Photo Tools
Sky Safari
Stellarium
The Photographer's Ephemeris
Weather Underground

INDEX

7
750 method, 115, 116

A
Accessories
    Batteries, 19, 69
    Battery grip, 19, 69, 100
    Bubble level, 22, 47, 112, 114
    Dew heater, 22
    Equatorial mount, 8, 17, 65-66, 71, 130-132
    Filters, 21-22, 64, 67, 83, 88, 123, 135
        Color filters (for flashlights), 83, 88
        Fog filters, 22, 135
        Graduated ND filter, 123-124
        Neutral density filter, 67
        Polarizer, 67
        Star filter, 22, 64
    Flashlights, 24-25, 45-46, 55, 82-84
    Headlamps, 24-25, 86-87, 91
    Laser pointer, 55
    LED panels, 84-86
    Lens cleaning cloth, 22-23
    Leveling base, 112
    Memory cards, 19
    Navigational tools, 25, 94
    Polar scope, 131-132
    Remote shutter releases / intervalometers, 19-21, 65, 69, 91, 98, 103, 114
    Robotic camera mount, 112
    Strobe lights, 45, 86
    Survival gear, 25
Airglow, 45, 75, 117, 139
Airplane lights, 70-71
Alaska photos,
    Fairbanks, 47
    Wiseman, 14, 23, 35, 51, 73, 114-115, 136
Android apps
    Aurora Alert, 73
    Aurora Buddy, 73
    DSLR Remote, 32
    Photo Tools, 32, 57, 101
    Sky Safari, 32
Andromeda Galaxy, 6, 7-8, 36
Arizona photos, 27, 64, 66, 92, 106
Astrophotography, 130

B
Belt of Venus, 38
Bioluminescence, 79
Black card technique, 123-124
Blending multiple exposures, 9, 22, 45, 46, 53, 63, 65, 66, 81, 88, 101-109, 123-135

C
California, Mission Bay, 79
Camera settings
    Aperture, 49, 72, 98-100, 101, 103-104, 113, 126
    Built-in level, 22
    Focusing, 53-57, 97-98, 132, 134
        Depth of field, 13-16, 32, 42, 43, 49, 56-57, 103-104, 111, 112, 123, 126, 132
        Hyperfocal distance, 32, 56-57, 132
    High ISO Noise Reduction, 60-61
    Histogram, 53, 72, 74, 77
    Interval timer, 20-21, 69, 103
    ISO, 11, 12, 51-52, 69, 72, 74, 77, 78, 88, 101, 104, 124, 125, 140
    LCD screen, 52, 53, 54, 56, 58, 90, 104, 124
    Live View, 54, 55
    Long Exposure Noise Reduction, 59-60, 93, 100, 101, 103, 109, 114, 124, 125, 129, 130, 150
    Mirror lock-up, 65, 103
    RAW / JPEG, 58, 60-61, 138
    Rule of 500, 50-51, 63, 72, 78, 113, 124, 125, 150
    Self-timer, 20, 91, 103
    Shutter speed, 49-51, 74, 77, 98, 101-103, 135
    White balance, 57-58, 61, 138-139

Appendix

Cameras,
    Digital cameras, 8, 11-12
    Film cameras, 8, 12, 96-100, 109
Canada photos, 10, 40, 58, 61, 73, 113
Celestial Equator, 96
Clothing
    Hand and foot warmers, 22, 23
    Heat Factory Pop-Top Mittens, 23
    Merino wool, 23
    NEOS Overshoes, 24
    Verseo ThermoGloves, 23-24
Colorado photos
    Alamosa, 62, 72
    Hovenweep Nat'l Monument, 34
    Mayflower Gulch, 44
    Mount Bross, 87
    Mushroom Rocks, 128
    Paradise Divide, 118-119
    Pawnee National Grasslands, 28-29, 99
    Rocky Mountain National Park, 70
Comets, 71, 131
Constellations, 22, 36, 68, 69, 134, 147, 149
    Big Dipper (Ursa Major), 43, 68, 93-94, 134
    Cassiopeia, 94
    Orion, 36, 43, 68, 91, 134
Costa Rica photos, 96, 110

D
Dinoflagellates, 79

E
Earth's shadow, 38
Eclipses,
    Lunar, 32, 65-66, 131, 135
    Solar, 32, 66-67

F
Firefly Squid, 79
Focus stacking, 15, 42, 46, 49, 56, 60, 85, 86, 111, 132-133, 152
Forest fires, 53, 77-78

G
Golden Mean, 46

H
Hawaii photos, 18, 76-77

I
Iceland photos, 1, 73, 74, 76, 89
Indonesia, 76
International Space Station, 71
Italy, 76
iTunes apps
    3D Sun, 73
    Aurora Forecast, 73
    PhotoPills, 32, 57, 101

J
Japan, Toyoma Bay, 79

L
Lava, 18, 53, 76-77
Leading lines, 46
Lens aberrations
    Chromatic aberration, 13, 55, 105, 142
    Coma, 13, 49, 113, 116
    Distortion, 142
    Vignetting, 13, 103, 116, 117, 119, 131, 142, 147
Lenses, 12-18
    Parfocal lenses, 54
    Varifocal lenses, 54, 55
Light painting, 20, 81-91, 102, 147, 152
Light pollution, 27-28, 31-32, 33, 44-45, 75, 149
Lightning, 20, 21, 59, 62, 71-72, 78, 79

M
Magellanic Clouds, 36
Maldives, Vaadhoo Island, 79
Meteor showers
    Geminids, 36, 68, 70
    Leonids, 68
    Perseids, 37, 68
    Radiant, the 69-71
Meteors, 20, 32, 59, 68-71, 81
Milky Way, 6, 7, 16, 27, 28-29, 32, 33, 36-37, 39, 41, 43, 45, 54, 60, 67, 81, 84,

85, 111, 116, 117, 120-121, 122, 123, 125, 134, 138, 139, 144, 148, 151
Moon, 7, 27-28, 32, 33-36, 38, 39, 42, 44, 49, 51, 53, 54, 63-66, 67, 68, 75, 78, 81, 90, 91, 98-100, 101, 103, 104, 108-109, 123, 124, 135, 139, 143
Moonbows, 78, 79

N

New Jersey, Manasquan Beach, 79
New Zealand, Waitomo Caves, 79
Night vision, 9, 25, 78
Noctilucent clouds, 75-76
Noise, 8, 11, 33, 34, 36, 49, 58-61, 63, 104, 111, 124, 127, 141-142, 143-144, 146, 149-150, 153
    Dark frames, 59, 101, 104, 105, 106, 108, 124, 125, 130, 131, 150
    Dark noise, 59-60, 93, 100, 101, 103, 109, 124, 125, 129, 130, 141, 150
    Flat frames, 131
    Photon noise, 59-61, 125, 141
    Offset/bias frames, 131
    Read noise, 61, 131
North Star, 32, 71, 93-94, 96, 131
Northern lights, 10, 14, 23, 35, 40, 47, 51, 53, 58, 61, 73-75, 89, 111, 112, 113, 114-115, 136
Norway, 73

P

Papua New Guinea, 76
Parallax, 111
People, including, 45, 91
Planetary conjunctions, 32, 68
Planets
    Earth, 7, 28-29, 36, 38, 64, 66, 67, 68, 93, 130
    Jupiter, 7, 38, 39, 68, 109
    Mars, 68, 135
    Mercury, 68
    Neptune, 7, 68
    Saturn, 68
    Uranus, 68
    Venus, 7, 37, 38, 39, 68, 109, 138

Post-processing techniques
    Black and white conversion, 151-152
    Blending exposures, 123-135
    Curves adjustments, 145
    Dodging and burning, 84, 90, 127, 146-147, 149, 151
    Enlarging star size, 133-135, 147-149
    Focus stacking, 132-133
    HDR images, 123
    Lens corrections, 142
    Levels adjustments, 144
    Lightroom adjustments, basic, 138-140
    Luminosity masks, 127, 139, 144-145, 146, 147, 148, 153
    Minimizing light pollution, 149
    Minimizing star trails, 150-151
    Noise reduction, 141-142, 143-144, 149-150
    Sharpening, 141, 152-153
    Star trails, 104-108
    Stitching images, 116-121
    Vibrance / saturation, 145-146
Proxima Centauri, 7
Puerto Rico, Mosquito Bay, 79

R

Reciprocity failure, 100, 101
Rule of thirds, 46-47

S

Satellites, 70-71
Sirius, 36, 68
Software programs
    Advanced Stacker Plus, 108
    Astronomy Tools Actions Set, 22, 108
    Auto Pano Pro, 120-121
    DeepSkyStacker, 131
    Floris Van Bruegel's script, 104-105, 106
    Google Earth, 28-29
    HDR Efex Pro, 123
    Helicon Focus, 133
    Hugin, 120
    Lightroom, Adobe, 9, 59-60, 61, 104-106, 116-118, 137, 138-143, 151-152, 153
    Magic Lantern, 20, 103

Microsoft ICE, 119-120
Nik Sharpener Pro, 153
Nik Silver Efex Pro, 152
PhotoKit Sharpener, 152-153
Photographer's Ephemeris, The, 28
Photoshop, Adobe, 9, 59-60, 63-64, 71, 104, 106, 107-108, 118-119, 121, 125-126, 127, 128, 129-130, 131, 132-133, 134, 135, 137, 138, 140, 143-153
PT Gui, 121
Sam Waguila's script, 108
Star Spikes Pro, 22, 108, 149
StarStax, 108
Startrails.exe, 107
Stellarium, 27-28, 67, 120
Topaz DeNoise, 61, 142, 143-144
Southern lights, 73
Star trails, 12, 15, 20, 27, 32, 36, 49, 59, 60, 78, 93-109, 150-151
   Comet-like star trails, 107-108
   Moon trails, 64, 101, 108-109
Starry Nights Calendar, 32
Stitched images, 8, 14-16, 47, 59, 74-75, 85, 86, 111-121, 122, 127-129, 130, 131, 147
Sunspots, 73, 75
Sunstar effect, 63-64, 67

T
Tides, 39
Tripods
   Legs, 18
   Ball heads, 18-19, 112, 114-115, 116
   Panoramic heads, 111, 115
   3-way pan/tilt heads, 112, 115, 132
Twilight, 138
   Astronomical, 39, 126, 128, 139
   Civil, 37-38, 65, 75, 126
   Nautical, 39, 65, 104

U
United Kingdom, Norfolk
Utah photos
   Arches Nat'l Park, 12, 20, 38, 50, 55, 69, 82, 95, 98, 101, 105, 109, 116, 117, 120-121, 133, 138, 141, 144, 146, 148, 151, 221
   BLM lands, 3, 16, 39, 45, 56, 64, 67, 85, 95, 134, 135
   Bryce Canyon Nat'l Park, 129
   Canyon Rims Rec. Area, 48, 60, 80, 86, 102, 152
   Canyonlands Nat'l Park, 30, 91, 122, 125, 126, 127
   Capitol Reef Nat'l Park, 24
   Castle Valley, 79
   Escalante Nat'l Monument, 33, 43, 94
   Goblin Valley State Park, 54
   Hovenweep Nat'l Monument, 34
   La Sal Mountains, 78
   San Rafael Swell, 6, 57, 97

V
Vanuatu, 76
Vietnam, Halong Bay, 79
Virgin Islands photos, 37
Volcanoes, 76-77, 96, 110

W
Websites
   Astronomy Calendar, 32
   Clear Dark Sky, 31
   DxOMark, 11
   DOF Master, 57
   Light Pollution Atlas, 31-32
   Tides Online, 39
   Volcano Discovery, 76
   Weather Underground, 30-31

Z
Zodiacal light, 37, 75, 81

REFERENCES

Allister Benn's *Seeing the Unseen*
http://harvestinglight.net/

David Kingham's *Night Tutorials*
http://www.davidkingham.com/blog/keyword?k=night+tutorials

Floris Van Breugel's *The Twilight Hour*
http://www.artinnaturephotography.com/gallery/twilightarticle/

Ian Norman's *Lonely Speck*
http://www.lonelyspeck.com

Jeffrey Sullivan's blog
http://www.jeffsullivanphotography.com/

Mike Berenson's *Articles & Tutorials*
http://www.coloradocaptures.com/night-photography-blog/cat/how-to-articles-tutorials

Mikko Lagerstedt's *How to Process Star & Night Sky Pictures in Lightroom 5 & Photoshop*
http://www.mikkolagerstedt.com/blog/2013/11/8/night-photography-tutorial-lightroom-5-photoshop

Nat Coalson's *Nature Photography Photo Workshop* and *Lightroom 5*
http://www.natcoalson.com/instruction/books/

Phil Hart's blog
http://www.philhart.com/

Royce Bair's *Into the Night Photography*
http://intothenightphoto.blogspot.com/

Steven Christenson's *Star Circle Academy*
http://starcircleacademy.com/

Thomas O'Brien's *Your Guide To Photographing A Meteor Shower*
http://iso.500px.com/meteor-shower-tips/

Todd Salat's *Predicting the Aurora Borealis*
http://www.aurorahunter.com/aurora-prediction.php

Tony Kuyper's *Tutorials & Luminosity Masks*
http://goodlight.us/writing/tutorials.html

Tony Prower's *Magic Cloth Technique*
http://icelandaurora.com/blog/2010/07/20/tonys-magic-cloth-technique/